CROSS-OVER DESIGN

THE VISUAL PLAY SERIES

NEWWEBPICK.COM
SUPER PICK OF THE WORLD

CYPI PRESS

Crossover Design

Author: NewWebPick Team

Project Editors: Guang Guo, Yvonne Zhao, Xiaoqiang Yi

Copy Editor: Jones Gregory Fay

Book Designer: Jing Yu

First published in the United Kingdom in March 2009 by
CYPI PRESS

Add: 79 College Road, Harrow Middlesex, Greater
London, HA1 1BD, UK

Tel: +44 (0) 20 3178 7279

Fax: +44 (0) 20 3002 4648

E-mail: sales@cypi.net   editor@cypi.net

Website: www.cypi.co.uk

ISBN: 978-0-9560453-0-0

Printed in China

Preface

An athlete may also be a singer, and a rock singer may still be a French chef. A driver who does not want to be a chef would not be a good tailor...

I believe that everyone has a lot of expertise, especially designers.

In their innate ways of thinking, designers are creative thinkers, different from ordinary people, and so can give our lives more and more fun. Although they have lots of new ideas every day, they always serve a number of commercial customers, who need only to be provided with some kinds of design. Therefore, designers have to prevent themselves from falling into the trap of designing like a machine. Their spare time should be engaged in the designs of different categories. That would allow them to have an unusual experience, which would be the dream of their working status as a designer.

Graphic designers may also produce CG animation, industrial designers may paint graffiti on the street, and architects may be DJ experts...

Freedom, this is the pursuit of all mankind. For designers, that would have a more deep-rooted meaning beyond the life of the physical body.

Whatever type of designer you are, this book will help you find the design you love. Let us draw closer to the creative feelings of 24 designers from all over the world - the feelings of their genius designs behind the works, and also the feelings of a new way in their pursuit of freedom.

Let the 4,000,000 global NewWebPick designers read it with you: Crossover Design!

NewWebPick Team

G Graphic design
I Illustration design
S Space Design
M Multimedia Design
W Web Design
D Doll design
P Product Design
Gf Graffiti
Ph Photograph

LUCAS LASNIER

Can you please briefly tell us when and how you started "crossover" design? Also how "crossover" design impacted your design style and beliefs at work?

After five years working for different agencies and studios we felt the need to stop producing for others and start our own work, without boundaries and conditions. As a result, we started exploring different styles and mix them without shame. Therefore, we understood that the combination of techniques, styles, and languages enrich our own brand and design studio. The impact was strong enough to start breaking structures not only in the way we work but also in the way we encourage a new product and develop it.

What is your view of the current trend of "crossover" design? For example, Will the emergence of "crossover" design make the current separation of work boundaries fuzzy? Why? Will "crossover" affect the professionalism of design work?

We are constantly looking for new languages and tendencies. I think it is crucial that the graphic languages constantly change and every one of them can provide new features over that language. Limits at work became confusing when the idea to communicate is not clear or there is no explicit information of the work to do.

What is your work plan in the future?

For the future we would like to publish an illustrated story book on an animated DVD.

Name: Lucas Lasnier
Company: Kid Gaucho
Country: Argentina
Email: info@kidgaucho.com
lucas.lasnier@kidgaucho.com
website: http://www.kidgaucho.com

Bio:
Kid Gaucho is a project that emerged in Buenos Aires in 2002, headed by Lucas Lasnier and Andres Bonavera, both graphic designers and illustrators. Both Lucas and Andres are part of a generation fed on new aesthetic parameters, more versatile and anxious, expressed in cultural facts like the scene skater, the arrival of MTV in Latin America or street art. One of their distinctive qualities is their ability to create these new visual elements into the communication of an original and effective idea that highlights their commitment to the message that is transmitted. During its five years in the market, Kid Gaucho has been using several support resources (walls, animation, web, fabrics) to generate its own contents capable of exceeding the common places that a trend or vogue can impose. Their proposal is to address design through a multidisciplinary approach. The creative proposal of this project is to express their ideas in several languages (Illustration, painting, animation, calligraphy) and work tools to define a dynamic and versatile approach that works both in the commercial and experimental areas. This creative style is expressed in four essential areas of work: Direction of Art, Brand Image, Graphic Design, and Animation.

←···
Title: **Space Pulpo**
Medium: **Acrylic on paper**

Title: **Kid Gaucho Characters Poster**
Medium: **Vector illustration**

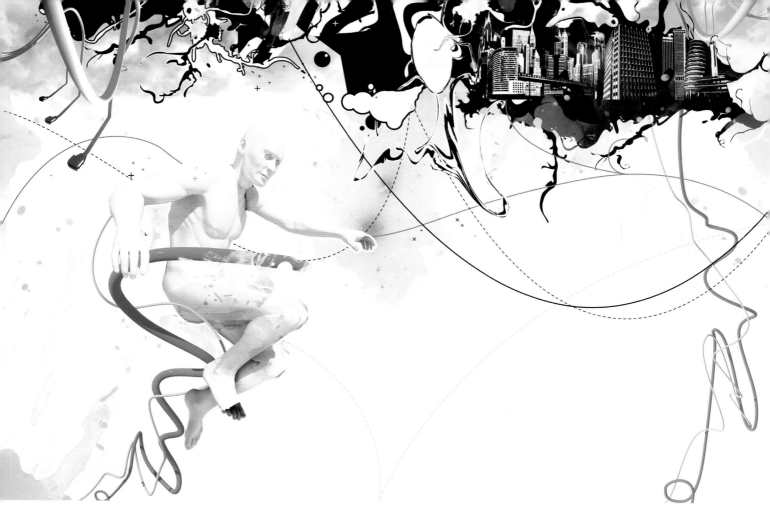

Title: **Dasani Enviroment**
Medium: **2D / 3D illustrations**

 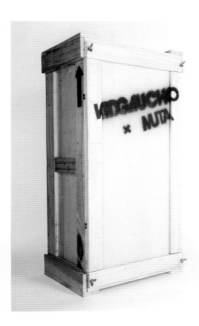 

Title: **Kid Gaucho Characters Poster**
Medium: **Vector illustration**

Title: **Customized stand for the Buenos Aires Fashion Week 2006**
Medium: **Sprays can / Stickers/ Papers / Stencils**

Title: **Dasani Enviroment**
Medium: **2D / 3D illustrations**

⋮

Title: **Design and illustrations for Hintmag**
Medium: **Illustrations and digital composition**

TSB / TechStyleBoard   HipHop4Freedom / TSB

TSB / TechStyleBoard

◄···
Title: **Help the box meet the globe**
Medium: **3D object / Wood manufactured / Glass /Hand painted**

⋮
Title: **Customized stand for the Buenos Aires Fashion Week 2006**
Medium: **Sprays can / Stickers/ Papers / Stencils**

↕
Title: **Mural street art Buenos Aires**
Medium: **Latex paint on wall**

←···
Title: **Custom store for complete girls clothes brand**
Medium: **Latex on walls**

···→
Title: **The Ramones**
Medium: **Acrylic on canvas**

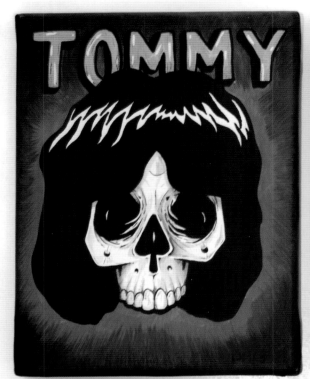

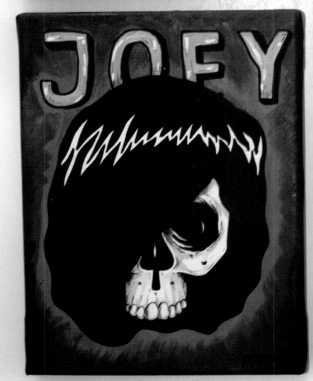

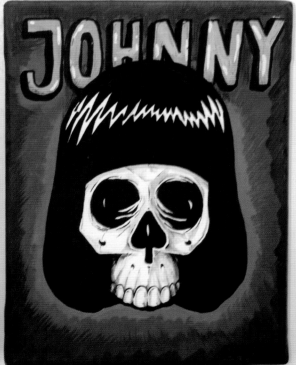

Title: **Custom store for complete girls clothes brand**
Medium: **Latex on walls**

...▸
Title: **Mural street art Buenos Aires / Electric plant**
Medium: **Latex on walls**

◄···
Title: **Timmy o' Tool video clip**
Medium: **For TV**

.·¹
Title: **Adidas Woman**
Medium: **Motion graphic spot**

···►
Title: **Adidas Originals**
Medium: **Motion graphic spot**

JAN LILIENTHAL.PAUTSCH

Can you please briefly tell us when and how you started "crossover" design? Also how "crossover" design impacted your design style and beliefs at work?

During the late 1990s, I created different interventional and spatial works, which were solely based on graphical, context-related structures. Working as a digital creative in advertising for over eight years now, however, I have been able to collaborate on a broad range of high profile interactive design projects and campaigns. In my current position as Creative Director at Argonauten G2 [Grey Global Group] in Berlin, I develop and supervise digital campaigns for various big brand clients. Within the scope of global campaigns, we cooperate closely with agencies all over the world, such as London-based Mother and AKQA, Wieden+Kennedy in Amsterdam, North Kingdom in Stockholm as well as PSYOP and Ogilvy & Mather in New York. Most recent campaigns for brands such as Red Coke [the Coke side of life] and Fanta [Play on!] provide an ideal playground for a variety of artistic influences, experimentation and interpretation. Hence, I enjoy having the great opportunity to be able to combine my personal art projects, past or future, with concepts for commercial applications. Both areas overlap and benefit from one another. Artistic gestures assist in various ways to solve conceptual problems of campaigns, and vice versa. In retrospect, it's the artistic legacy of Andy Warhol, the godfather of 'crossover' design.

What is your view of the current trend of "crossover" design? For example, will the emergence of "crossover" design make the current separation of work boundaries fuzzy? Why? Will "crossover" affect the professionalism of design work?

Recent design projects, especially in the field of interactive media, have never been more exciting and highly professional. Street art, spatial works, and motion design are constantly bursting the limits of traditional forms of art reception. At the same time, the fine line between artist and designer is dissolving. 2D skills are moving into the 3D realm. We are about to enter a new dimension, and recent campaigns by, for example, Sony Bravia and Adidas as well as outstanding and trend-setting realizations by Paranoid (Paris), PSYOP (N.Y.) or North Kingdom (Stockholm) signify that artistic and campaign strategies increasingly meld and thus give way to new and once more challenging ideas and advanced standards for high profile (interactive) design work. Even the most perfect work of art, no matter what its context, is always driven by a desire for illusion, while, at the same time, being in conflict with its own mortality. This is Mortal Magic.

Name: Jan Lilienthal.Pautsch
Company: MRTLMGYC [ThisMortalMagic™]
Country: Germany
Email: hit@ThisMortalMagic.com
website: www.ThisMortalMagic.com

Bio:
MRTLMGYC [ThisMortalMagic™] Label and showcase of Jan Lilienthal.Pautsch, Creative Director, lives and works in Berlin. Conceptual work, design direction, executions and artistic projects. Full profile available under: www.ThisMortalMagic.com
Clients:
Bacardi, Bertelsmann Group, Coca-Cola Germany, the Coca-Cola Company, Lowe Communication Group, Beiersdorf, Swatch, Toshiba, VW.
Awards: DDC / DDP / FAB / FWA / IF / NEO / NYf / One Show
Recognition: Annual Multimedia / PAGE / Selection / VISUAL-X / Who's Who in Design
Broadcasts: fcukstar / GommaR / NewstodayR / NewWebPick / spyline / TOCAM

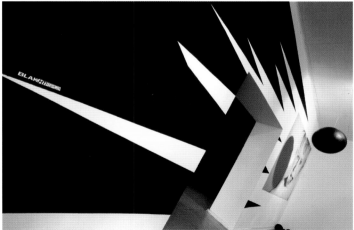

Title: **The black hit of space**
Medium: **Spatial work, environment, foto [200x300 cm], acrylic on wall, balls**
Credits and Rationale:

A collaboration between Jan Lilienthal. Pautsch, Veysel Oender [Amok] and Roman Maerz, as part of Backjumps - The Live Issue #3, Urban Communication und Aesthetics, Kunstraum Kreuzberg/ Bethanien, Berlin. "THE BLACK HIT OF SPACE is an experiment, an experimental design set up in order to find out what emerges from the close collaboration between a photographer, an ex-writer, and an artist. What happens, if three individual forms of artistic expression co-occupy a space? And, what if the title THE BLACK HIT OF SPACE serves as the inspiration to the project? The outcome is a room-encompassing installation - both attacking and absorbing. An interplay of forces that distinctively continues in our further projects."BLAKHTFSP3 TheBlackHitOfSpace™]Participating Artists and Projects amongst others: ASH [Copenhagen/Paris], Blu [Bologna], Dave the Chimp [London], SKKI [Paris], ZEVS [Paris].

...▸

Title: **MRTLMGYC screenshots**
Medium: **One Page Portfolio, HTML/Flash**
Credits and Rationale:
Current showcase and home base of Jan Lilienthal.Pautsch. Conceptual work, design direction, campaign executions and artistic projects.

◂...

Title: **Drehen/Wenden turning tricks**
Medium: **Offspace occupation: videoloops, plots**
Credits and Rationale:
An office space is turned into a glass showcase, with two different photo-sessions as well as two video projections screened on the outer surface of the large scale windows facing a busy street. During the day, each of the photo-sessions displays a set of stills of a uniformed character occupying diverse positions towards the camera/spectator. At night, the window surface serves as a cinematic screen. The video is projected upside down, showing the same character as before in the photographs, now sitting on an office chair while rotating in high speed around him - over-and-over again, to the left and to the right. Front of Haus Pietzsch, Unter den Linden, Berlin.

‹···
Title: **Science Fiction**
Medium: **Audiovisual installation: helium filled, illuminated ball, ticker projection, sound**
Credits and Rationale:
The full moon above the glass box, as well as the hoarse electronic voice of the computer brain from Godard's film 'Alphaville', that calls out every so often, both combine with the architecture of the technical monument– 'Science Fiction or moon above the Kurfurstendamm' delivers an absurd statement on the hype and glamour that determined the turn of the twentieth century and, at the same time, initiates a romantic element to the omnipresent take-over of power through electrical machines and devices."
Dr. Ute Tischler, curator Group show: countdown west 2k, Berlin.

···›
Title: **On Assignment**
Medium: **Moods**
Credits and Rationale:
Pitch comps in combination with a quote from Stefan Sagmeister:
"We should be designing coke bottles, postal trucks and huge commercial web sites instead of leaving those jobs [which really do have cultural impact] to the marketing/branding idiots." Quote: TWEEDLEDEETWEEDLEDUM. My year of graphic design without clients, Stefan Sagmeister. In: GRAPHIC 10.

What is your work plan in the future?

In my position as Creative Director I get the opportunity to work with a host of great local and international major brand clients who operate in a range of diverse and exciting areas and for whom we, my team and I, develop creative concepts and campaigns. Innovative dynamic and powerful tools such as 3D and the motion aspect, illustration, as well as storytelling and narrative aspects in general will become more and more important. In order to be able to meet these high standards we always need some more good people.

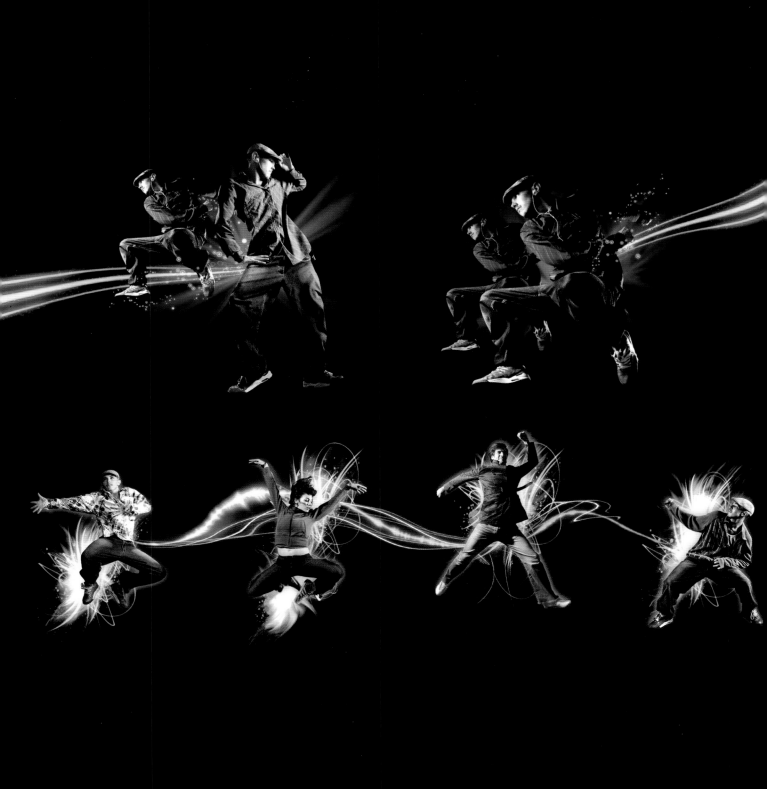

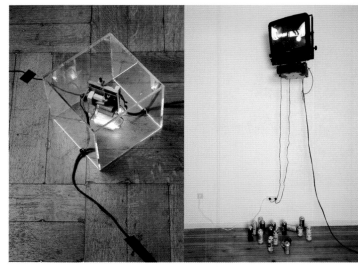

<···↑

Title: **This Mortal Magic**

Medium: **Audiovisual installations: spatial works, machines, models**

Credits and Rationale:

"**The magic that derives from electronic devices within the process of creating reality - including art – is reduced on the surface and, eventually, obliterated. Taking apart the object's visual and functional integrity, the artist equally causes the disappearance of some sort of semantic profile. Lilienthal's cut' isolates the spectator from the visual experience by using a rewind-mode. One can't see, or can hardly see, anything. At this crucial point, the artist [such as Siegfried and Roy] tries to catch all the people within the audience who do not believe in magic.**" Dr. Ute Tischler, curator.

···›

Title: **Sensory Amazement! Fanta Global Toykit. A digital pick-and choose assortment**

Medium: **Digital Toykit, story-telling campaign**

Agency: **Argonauten G2, Berlin**

Client: **The Coca-Cola Company**

Job: **Creative Direction**

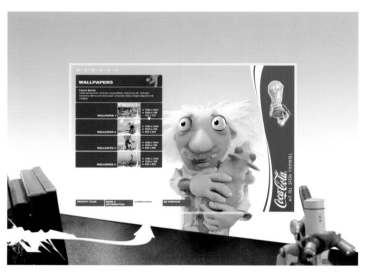

Title: **WE ALL SPEAK FOOTBALL**

Medium: **Marketing Platform, Online Campaign**

Agency: **Argonauten G2, Berlin**

Client: **The Coca-Cola Company**

Job: **Creative Direction**

Credits and Rationale:

Campaign challenge: design and development of the global Coca-Cola online campaign as part of the global iCoke Project, FIFA WM™ 2006. 10 modules, 60 markets, 11 languages.

Campaign objective: setup Coke as Fan-Brand No. 1 at FIFA WM™ 2006.

Campaign execution: In content and design, the campaign focuses on the fan and his-or-her boundless enthusiasm for the football world cup. Employing a visual language that is both highly aesthetical and emotional – though strictly renouncing the application of common national clichés – enables a straightforward multi-ethnic approach. that appreciates the worldwide attention and global passion for the sport.

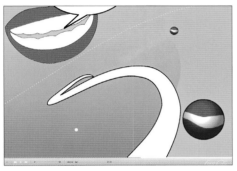

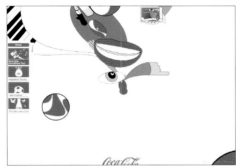

Title: **Life Meets Digital! Online Identity for the Coke Music Activation Germany**
Medium: **Brand Site, Online Campaign. cokesideoflife.de**
Agency: **Argonauten G2, Berlin**
Client: **Coca-Cola Germany**
Job: **Creative Direction**

Credits and Rationale:

Campaign challenge: Coke presents a digital stage for Grassroot bands. Music lovers rate their favorite bands. Campaign objective: Synthesis of international newcomer bands and their fans, including bands such as Maximo Park, Paolo Nutini, Adam Green. Core Idea: Infecting others with the joy of music.
Campaign executions: Interactive and state-of-the-art Coke Music Player with special music program and User generated content [Cooperation with AKQA, London]. Staging of the key visual [Mother, London] as a 3D splash. Life Meets Digital!

JANINA BÜCKING
BEST FRIENDS

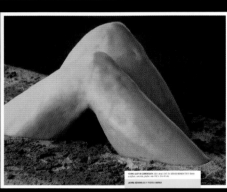

UNTITLED 2002
directed photography: foto Heiko Prigge

JANINA BÜCKING BEST FRIENDS WORKS

CONCRETE HEAD 2004, Berlin
performance

JANINA BÜCKING BEST FRIENDS WORKS

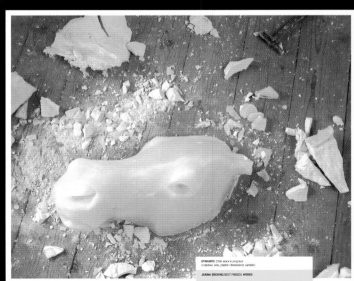

DYNAMITE 2006 work in progress
sculpture, wax, plaster; dimensions variable;

JANINA BÜCKING BEST FRIENDS WORKS

‹···

Title: **Best Friends**
Medium: **Online Portfolio.**
janinabuecking.com
Credits and Rationale:
Portfolio design for Janina
Buecking, artist, Berlin.
BEST FRIENDS is a series of
recent work investigating
subconscious desires repressed
in personal identity.

⋮

Title: **IdN 15**
Medium: **Comp**
Credits and Rationale:
Competition/Contribution: WE
ARE ALL CONNECTED / IdN 15th
Anniversary.

Can you please briefly tell us when and how you started "crossover" design? Also how "crossover" design impacted your design style and beliefs at work?

I began my graphic life with graffiti. Then my training in the school of applied art opened me up in many ways. I am naturally interested by all which is related with the image, be it near or far. So the drawing, the photography, the sculpture, etc are for me tools which express my graphic thought. Actually, I tend to focus on drawing and painting, which are my favorite areas, but I keep an eye on the other creative areas as well.

What is your view of the current trend of "crossover" design? For example, will the emergence of "crossover" design make the current separation of work boundaries fuzzy? Why? Will "crossover" affect the professionalism of design work?

I think that the mixture can really be enriching. However there is a risk: mixing everything can damage the legibility of a project. And especially badly mixing domains could render this mixture hard to understand.

What is your work plan in the future?

As I told you before I turn more to hand-made things, such as drawing and painting on canvas. But I keep a contact with graphic design through my teaching job and my work in the agency.

Name: Olivier Menanteau / moon
Company: moon
Country: France
Email: moon@mxtr.org
Blog: http://moon-mixtur.blogspot.com/
Website: http://www.mxtr.org/moon
Shop: http://moonshop.bigcartel.com

Bio:
Name: Olivier Menateau / Moon, 30, living in France. I am a free-lance graphic designer and at the same time a graphist /AD in a studio named "Fly designers." I also belong to "Mxtr", a group made of graphists, illustrators, and painters. Everything started 10 years ago, with graffiti. I was then trained in an"Art Applique School. "This training allowed me to explore different avenues of media expression. I practice drawing, numerical painting, paint on canvas, walls, customizing objects, video creation... This year, I began to teach graphic design in a school of applied art and communication.

‹···
Title: **Self-portrait**

‡ ···▸ ‡
Title: **A book with sketches**
Credits and Rationale:
**Order it at HYPERLINK "http://
www.lulu"http://www.lulu.
com/content/1151623**

Title: **Color Z**
Medium: **Color paper, pen on paper, + Photoshop**

Title: **White Splash Around My Head**
Medium: **Digital painting**

Title: **Ocre-et-gris**
Medium: **Acrylic on canvas**

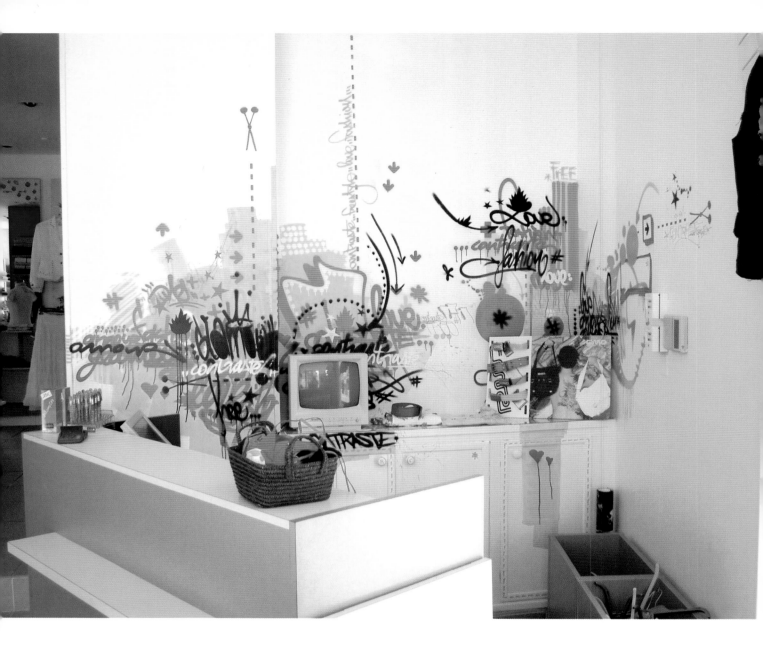

‡ ⋯▸
Title: **Interior-fashion shop**

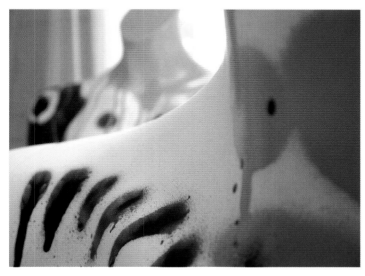

<... Title: **Graffiti-raisin**

...> Title: **Graffiti-pink flavour 2**

⋮ Title: **Graffiti-pink flavor**

COMALAB

G S M

Can you please briefly tell us when and how you started "crossover" design? Also how "crossover" design impacted your design style and beliefs at work?

There wasn't a precise moment when we decided to start doing crossover design, this happened spontaneously, due to our passion for our work and the continuing desire to experiment with new approaches to the design project. In our work crossover design has an important role, because it contributes to our daily projects.

What is your view of the current trend of "crossover" design? For example, will the emergence of "crossover" design make the current separation of work boundaries fuzzy? Why? Will "crossover" affect the professionalism of design work?

We think that the edge is very thin, and the two things go forward together, and besides we think that the crossover can only influence our design work in a positive way. Of course it's up to us to find a good balance.

What is your work plan in the future?

For the future we only have one goal: namely to continue to make good design.

Company Name: COMALAB
Country: Italy
Email: info@comalab.net
Web: www.comalab.net

Bio:
Comalab, born in 2005 from the minds of two young communication pros, is today one of the most active graphic agencies in Milan, which on a day-by-day basis confronts itself with some of the world's biggest working realities. At the root of Comalab's work ethic are the passion for communication projects and the constant striving to find different routes; Wallpaper and Stylelab, two in-house projects at Comalab, are perfect examples of how this young agency presents itself to alternative scenarios. The enthusiasm for getting involved in new creative adventures allows the team to operate in a variety if different sectors of design utilizing many mediums: exhibitions, branding, web, advertising, events and paper graphics are some of the components that reinforce Comalab's abilities. One sector that is developing at a higher rate than others is GUIs (graphic user interface) this area allows them to get involved with their clients most important brands within the technology sector which is focused on personal devices on an international level.

Title: **60's Living Room**

Title: **Lounge Bar**

Title: **Bedroom**

Title: **FM37 Print Advertising**

Title: **FM37 Interface**

Title: **FM37 Awards**

Title: **VAS Collection**

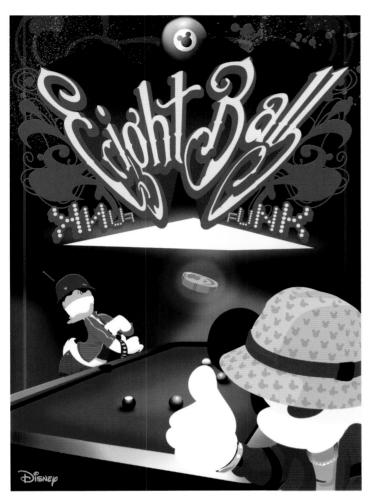

Title: **Eight Ball**

Title: **Street Girl**

Title: **VAS Collection**

MACIEJ HAJNRICH

Name: Maciej Hajnrich
Company: Valp
Country: Poland
Email: valp@valpnow.com
Website: www.valpnow.com

Can you please briefly tell us when and how you started "crossover" design? Also how "crossover" design impacted your design style and beliefs at work?

To be honest I realized the idea of crossover design when you asked me to take part in this book. I mean I wasn't thinking before that you could have design as a hobby which hasn't influenced your work lately. I was wrong – I was sketching every blank sheet of paper with little men doing weird things. Drawing isn't my main skill so it took about two years for me to decide to use it in my commercial works such as websites, which I haven't been designing recently. This is the best example I can give, but before that I was influenced by typography and photography (who isn't?) which was a very good experience and which I use every day.

What is your view of the current trend of "crossover" design? For example, will the emergence of "crossover" design make the current separation of work boundaries fuzzy? Why? Will "crossover" affect the professionalism of design work?

There are rules just to be broken, so nothing new will be the same. And that's why we should explore more; expand our horizons, mix media and ideas… Only then we will be able to reach new goals, and that's what is especially important now, when people say they have seen everything. Crossover design affects professionalism but in a positive way. It could be described through words, I've read about typography in posters: you can design a good poster with poor typo, but using good typography doesn't guarantee a good poster.

What is your work plan in the future?

This year will be really busy for me. I want to launch a new project (a kind of evolution of the 5 year old "Nietylko"), gain some funds for my own small studio for me and my fiancee which will be hopefully possible in 12 months, and then we can move to a new apartment. And last but not least, I am going to make my designs better.

Bio:
Maciej Hajnrich born in 1981, Poland. He is a graphic designer and illustrator.
When digital art was (just) a hobby he was an editor in several video games magazines. Since 2003 he has been working as a graphic designer and art director. He graduated in IT with basics of graphic design and multimedia in 2005. By 2003 he had gained enough experience to enable him to work full-time as a freelancer. Later he founded Valp.
"For me graphic design was always something more than just a profession. I want to play with the imagination, experiment with techniques and offer professional services because I believe it's the best way to make unique art."

Title: **Hariasen –Nietylko**

TRUST
THE
FUTURE
www.
thekdu.com
www.
nietylko.net

Title: **Trust the future**

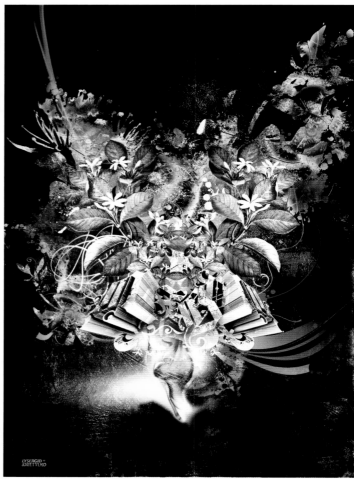

Title: **A Touch of Me**

Title: **Back from space**

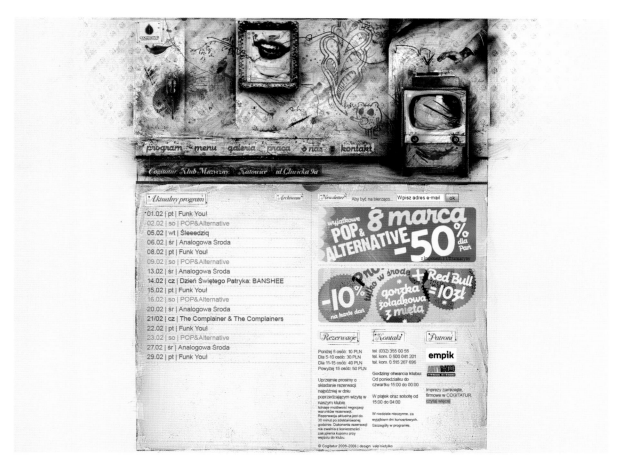

Title: **Beltaine's CD cover**

Title: **Cogitatur-web**

PACARABANU

design'07: www.nietylko.net

Title: **Last supper**

Title: **Proof7' Logo**

YONGIL LEE & BONGHEE KIM

<u>Can you please briefly tell us when and how you started "crossover" design?</u>
<u>Also how "crossover" design impacted your design style and beliefs at work?</u>

I would like to, first of all, describe my personal views of "crossover" design.
From the beginning of my career as a web designer, I have always thought that "crossover" design is a new evolutionary challenge. In other words, I see "crossover" design as an unavoidable process in the development of global history and culture as a whole, rather than regarding it as a simply recent trend in the web-related field. The basic concept of crossover, which may be defined as a combination of two different genres, has long been with us, just like the Austrian symbolist painter Gustav Klimtcreated a new genre in art known as "Art Nouveau," by combining art and textiles. In this modern world, being exposed to numerous designs, I believe that "crossover" design is truly a driving force of what could be called "creativeness," as it can create a new genre by combining various design advantages. Also, "crossover" design can be said that it is an indicator of a completely new type of design, which combines different genres.

<u>What is your view of the current trend of "crossover" design? For example,</u>
<u>will the emergence of "crossover" design make the current separation of work</u>
<u>boundaries fuzzy? Why? Will "crossover" affect the professionalism of design</u>
<u>work?</u>

As mentioned above, we are living in this modern world, exposed to numerous and various designs. The world requires more progressive and advanced designs than ever. Accordingly, "crossover" design has become an unavoidable challenge in design today. As an inevitable process in the development of the design industry, "crossover" design indicates a new model for design through continuous and ceaseless efforts. However, I don't think that "crossover" design is something anyone can do easily. It is because a successful "crossover" design is possible: only when you have a deep understanding of the merits/demerits of countless previous designs. In this respect, "crossover" design will require related experts to think in a more professional way and have a deeper understanding of the environment for more specialized works.

<u>What is your work plan in the future?</u>

We are in the midst of various types of media. The internet is a good example. AWG has prepared for "New Media Content," which can be presented through the internet only by grasping characteristics of the various media. New Media Content is both variable and dynamic and boasts an advantage of reflecting the stream of times more quickly than the content of any other media.

Name: Yongil Lee & Bonghee Kim
Company: Artworksgroup
Country: South Korea
Email: info@kidgaucho.com
Website: http://www.artworksgroup.net
http://www.awgcollection.net

Bios:
We are a specialized provider staffed with various experts under organic and integrated Total ID Consulting which are needed for your special and diverse environmental identity demand in advertisement.

Title: **Justice-Boy**
Credits and Rationale:
The character of Justice Boy (JB) was created with my desire to reconcile with the world through his aggressive, but lovely invectiveness. You will hear about JB in various interesting stories.

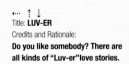
Title: **LUV-ER**

Credits and Rationale:

Do you like somebody? There are all kinds of "Luv-er" love stories.

53

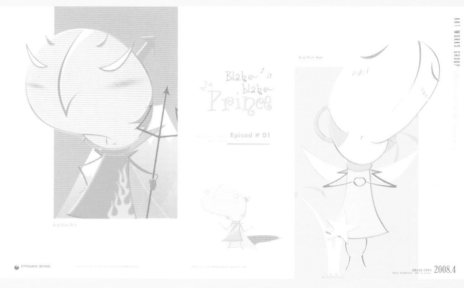

Title: **Blah Blah Prince**
Credits and Rationale:
The strange story of Blah Blah Prince.

Title: **LUV-ER**
Credits and Rationale:
Do you like somebody? There are all kinds of "Luv-er" love stories.

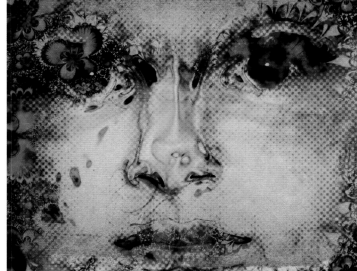

Title: **A fresco**

...▸

Title: **Spring & Girl**
Credits and Rationale:
Wake up ...girl.

Artworksgroup

AWG has pioneered the scope of the new design through the "Experimental Design and the Crossover of Media", while consistently striving for creativity and innovation.

WEBDESING

CHARACTER

ANIMATION

MOTION GRAPHIC

GRAPHIC

Title: **A fresco**

Title: **Fish**

Credits and Rationale:

**Expresses the passage of time
and thought.**

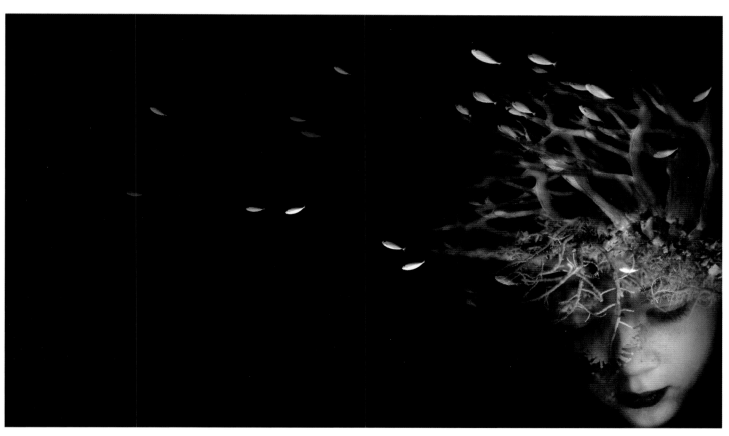

DIOGRAFIC

Can you please briefly tell us when and how you started "crossover" design? Also how "crossover" design impacted your design style and beliefs at work?

I have always been interested in the different areas of Design. My training is in Communications Design, which covers a range of areas such as Graphic Design, Web Design, Illustration, and Animation. This diverse base of training, combined with my natural interest in several areas of design, led me to the path of "crossover."For me it's very interesting to explore different areas and be able to combine them. The projects become dynamic, unique…

What is your view of the current trend of "crossover" design? For example, will the emergence of "crossover" design make the current separation of work boundaries fuzzy? Why? Will "crossover" affect the professionalism of design work?

I think that "crossover" design will gradually develop more. However, it is necessary to be careful with the simultaneous exploration in several areas, because it is difficult to have profound knowledge and keep up with the technical evolution in all areas, and this may affect the quality of the final work.

What is your work plan in the future?

Nowadays I am developing more works in the areas of Web Design and Illustration; most of my goals go down that path…Web design is for me the ideal work base because it gives me the freedom to explore and combine all of the areas where I like to work, it allows me to use and explore Motion Design, Graphic Design, Illustration... It's a very interactive and also dynamic area which is constantly changing, and that captivates me...

Name: Diografic
Country: Portugal
Email: mail@diografic.com
Web: www.diografic.com

Bio:
Diografic graduated with a degree in Communications Design from the Advanced School of Technology and Management in Portugal. He has worked as a designer for the digital marketing companies, "Six & Co (FullSix Group) ," "mEgo Company (United States)" and works on freelance Graphic Design, Illustration, Motion and Web Design projects. He has worked for international brands such as Martini, Burn, Samsung, and more. He is also a member of the Portuguese design collective, Ruadesign.net, whose goal is to optimize and promote Portuguese Design.

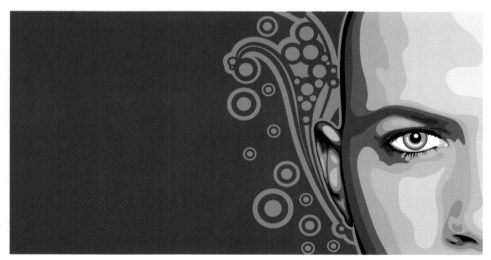

‹···
Title: **DioSelf**
Credits and Rationale: **Illustration for the "Ilustra-te", Illustration Exhibition by Etic in Lisbon, Portugal.**

Title: **Gentleman**
Credits and Rationale:
Illustration for Gentleman CD Cover

Title: **Logos**

Credits and Rationale:

Illustration for the "Mundo Mix 2007"

Title: **The Animals Aren't Dolls**
Credits and Rationale:
Illustration for the "Abrigo dos Animais Project"

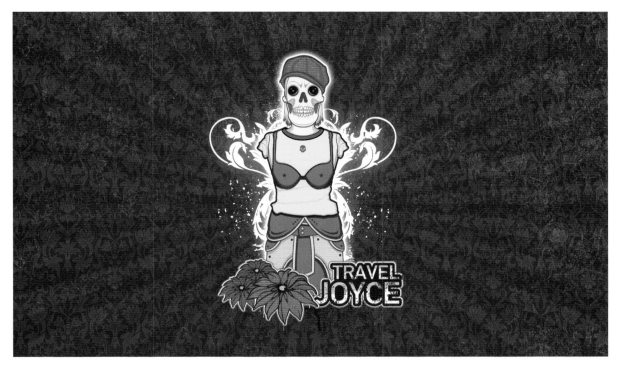

Title: **Travel Joyce**
Credits and Rationale:
Illustration for the Reinventa Event, Restart, Lisbon, Portugal.

← ⋯

Title: **Road**
Credits and Rationale:
Illustration for the "Mundo Mix 2007"

← ⋯

Title: **Sounds of Silence**
Credits and Rationale:
Illustration for the "Sounds of Silence" Website

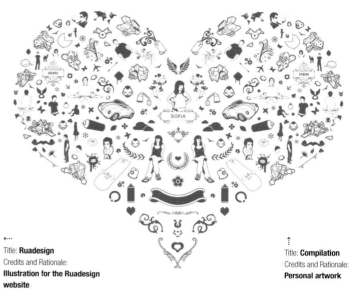

Title: **Ruadesign**
Credits and Rationale:
Illustration for the Ruadesign website

Title: **Compilation**
Credits and Rationale:
Personal artwork

Title: **The Seven Deadly Sins**
Credits and Rationale:
Illustrations for "Mangacurta" T-shirts

...›

Title: **Rebirth**
Credits and Rationale:
Illustration for the e-zine "Humus"

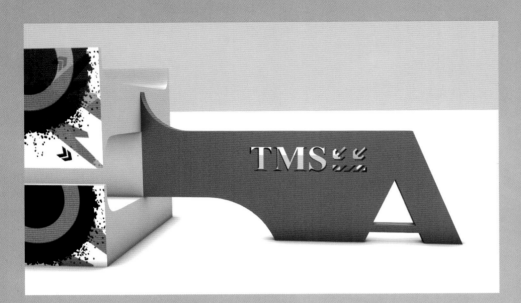

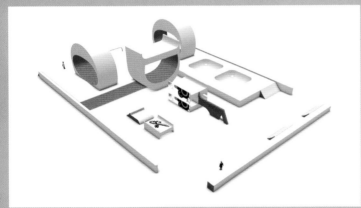

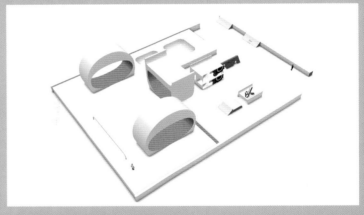

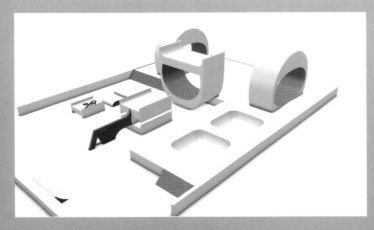

Title: **TimesPark**
Credits and Rationale:
Skate Park created with type.

Title: **Consume**
Credits and Rationale:
Flyer for an activity

HAMO STUDIO

Can you please briefly tell us when and how you started "crossover" design? Also how "crossover" design impacted your design style and beliefs at work?

We've always been involved with crossover design. From the first moment we decided to set up a studio we were going to produce crossover designs. Our studio is formed by designers from different areas and disciplines and we believe that the skills of each one feeds the way we understand design. We think it's totally necessary to feed our daily work.

What is your view of the current trend of "crossover" design? For example, will the emergence of "crossover" design make the current separation of work boundaries fuzzy? Why? Will "crossover" affect the professionalism of design work?

Yes. We think that crossover design affects every design field that encounters it. But not always in a bad way, we find lots of interesting pieces of work that are deemed crossover design and which inspires designers that are focused in one particular area. Nowadays we have access to so much information that anybody can produce really interesting works and you can watch it without leaving your desk, people can learn in an easier and faster way than before.

What is your work plan in the future?

We have many projects for the future, we're trying to expand our broadcast work and day by day we're getting more conscious about the great importance of personal and self promotion projects, it's in these types of works were we experiment, we learn, and which we enjoy the most.

Name: Pablo Sánchez
Company: Hamo Studio
Country: Spain
Email: pablo@hamo.es
Website: www.hamo.es

Bio:
Hamo Studio is a graphic design, illustration, motion graphics, and multimedia studio started in Barcelona in 2004. We enjoy communication and art in any of its variations. We all need to express ourselves, and Hamo does it using images. Images can be understood by the whole world, so Hamo Studio is the way for Borja Fuste, Ivan Cano and Pablo Sanchez to communicate with the world. You are not safe, everything and everybody inspires us.

Title: **Silas Lang**
Credits and Rationale:
CD artwork for the band Silas Lang

...▸

Title: **Freakstival**
Credits and Rationale:
Poster for the pop music festival Freakstival

Title: **Voices Underground Music Video**
Credits and Rationale:

Music video for the band Capsula and their track "Voices Underground". Recorded in Berlin and post-produced in Barcelona, "Voices Underground" is the 1st video clip from the album "Songs & Circuits" 2007.

Title: **Intendencies TV Identity**
Credits and Rationale:

Art direction, identity and motion graphics. Intendencies is a TV program.

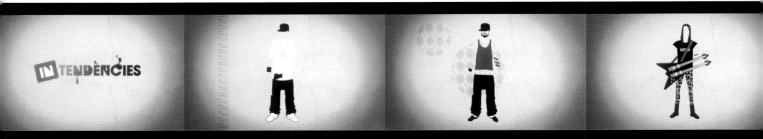

Title: **As time Breaks Off Music Video**
Credits and Rationale:

Music video "As Time Breaks Off" for the Delorean band. The video continues the disc concept: Into the Plateau. We decided to represent a trip from the city to the fields showing the growth and expansion of the big cities as we try to escape.

Title: **Gianduja Music Video**
Credits and Rationale:

Music video for the band The Linn Youki Project and their track "Gianduja". It's a new vision of the folk tale The Pied Piper of Hamelin. This video was chosen to participate in Resfest 10, in the Resfest Spain category.

Title: "Que esta passant!?" TV Identity
Credits and Rationale:
Art direction, identity and motion graphics. "Que esta passant!?" is a TV program.

Title: One More Sunday Music Video
Credits and Rationale:
Music video for the band Tokyo Sex Destruction, for the song "One More Sunday." Psychedelic, 70's poster forms and typographies are used in this video.

Title: Regresan de la Tumba Music Video
Credits and Rationale:
Music video for the song "Regresan de la tumba," for the The Tiki Phantoms. Direction, screenplay, and motiongraphics by Hamo Studio.

Title: Vulcan Music Video
Credits and Rationale:
First music video for the band Los Tiki Phantoms. The four disciples of Tiki God bring us their reverb fuelled instrumental surf 'n roll. This scary video presents the band with humour and in a B-movie style.

crash® VELOCIDAD NO ES SINONIMO DE PROGRESO

‹···
Title: **Logo**
Credits and Rationale:
Logo for illustration

‹···
Title: **Sakari**
Credits and Rationale:
Identity and T-shirt design for Sakari clothing. This brand, born in the Basque Country, offers an urban collection for men and women.

UNDERCODERS™
CREATIVE DEVELOPMENT TEAM

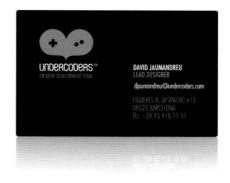

Title: **Undercoders**
Credits and Rationale:
**Identity for Undecoders. Creative
development team focused
on developing videogames on
different platforms.**

JAWA AND MIDWICH

Can you please briefly tell us when and how you started "crossover" design? Also how "crossover" design impacted your design style and beliefs at work?

Crossover design has always been an integral part of our creative practice. We find that using our illustration, typographic, and photographic skills enhances and enriches our graphic design solutions.

What is your view of the current trend of "crossover" design? For example, will the emergence of "crossover" design make the current separation of work boundaries fuzzy? Why? Will "crossover" affect the professionalism of design work?

On the whole crossover design is beneficial to the creative process and its use is widely seen around us every day which is a positive thing. There are some instances of certain disciplines being used with others by individuals who are not specifically trained in that field. This is detrimental to the idea of crossover design as the end results can look badly conceived and poorly executed.

What is your work plan in the future?

To continue experimenting.

Name: Simon Dovar / Nils Davey
Company: Jawa and Midwich
Country: UK
Email: info@jawa-midwich.com
Web: www.jawa-midwich.com

Bios:
Jawa and Midwich is an award winning graphic design studio providing design, illustration and art direction services for a wide variety of projects and clients that include music, branding culture, and film.

←···
Title: **Motorcitysoul 'Mango'**
Medium: **12" Record sleeve**
Credits and Rationale:
Our art direction for Motorcitysoul's new release combines elements of illustration and typography. Firstly we created our own typeface based loosely around Avant Garde Gothic letterforms. We then vectorised a floral print pattern and divided it through the typeface selectively deleting elements. The sleeve was printed in black and gold.

Title: **Better Than Nothing**

Medium: **Poster**

Credits and Rationale:

This promotional A2 poster was created purely from circles. Instead of trying to use a filter or computer aided technique to produce the circle effect Jawa and Midwich created and placed each circle individually. This illustrative technique, whilst time consuming, produced a striking illustration / typography crossover piece.

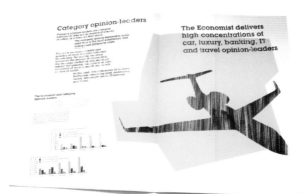

Title: **The Power of Influencers**

Medium: **A3 book**

Credits and Rationale:

Jawa and Midwich were commissioned by Brand Genetics and The Economist to create a brochure of market research information.

We created a super sized A3 brochure on thick paper stock with a combination of typography and illustration filled with handmade textures. We also adjusted the grid and typography to a 10° angle, making the entire document dynamically different.

‘The day of
the dead’

Above: 206 bones of the human
skeleton in size order.

Designed and illustrated
by Jawa and Midwich.

www.jawa-midwich.com

Axial skeleton			
Skull 22		**Vertebral Column 26**	
1-2	Parietal	30	Atlas (Cervical)
3	Occipital	31	Axis (Cervical)
4-5	Temporal	32-36	Cervical
6	Frontal	37-48	Thoracic
7-8	Zygomatic	49-53	Lumbar
9	Sphenoid	54	Sacrum x 5 fused
10-11	Lacrimal	55	Coccyx x 4 fused
12	Vomer		
13-14	Palatine	**Chest 25**	
15	Ethmoid	56-69	Vertebrosternal
16-17	Inferior Concha	70-75	Vertebrochondral
18-19	Nasal	76-79	Vertebral
20-21	Maxilla	80	Sternum
22	Mandible		
Ossicles 6			
23-24	Malleus		
25-26	Incus		
27-28	Stapes		
Hyoid 1			
29	Hyoid		

Appendicular skeleton			
Shoulder Girdle 4		**Legs 8**	
81-82	Scapula	147-148	Femur
83-84	Clavicle	149-150	Patella
		151-152	Tibia
Arms 6		153-154	Fibula
85-86	Humerus		
87-88	Radius	**Feet 52**	
89-90	Ulna	155-182	Phalanges
		183-192	Metatarsals
Hands 54		193-194	Cuboid
91-118	Phalanges	195-196	Lateral Cuneiform
119-128	Metacarpals	197-198	Intermediate Cuneiform
129-130	Hamate	199-200	Medial Cuneiform
131-132	Capitate	201-202	Calcaneus
133-134	Trapezoid	203-204	Navicular
135-136	Pisiform	205-206	Talus
137-138	Triquetrum		
139-140	Lunate		
141-142	Scaphoid		
143-144	Trapezium		
Pelvic Girdle 2			
145-146	Pelvic		

···▸

Title: **Day of the Dead**

Medium: **Poster**

Credits and Rationale:

**This promotional A2 poster
was created to showcase our
design and illustration skills
as well as convey information.
Jawa and Midwich researched
and collated information on all
the bones in the human body.
These were then illustrated and
scaled proportionally to each
other in size order. Finally the
illustrations were laid out with
typography to create a dynamic
composition.**

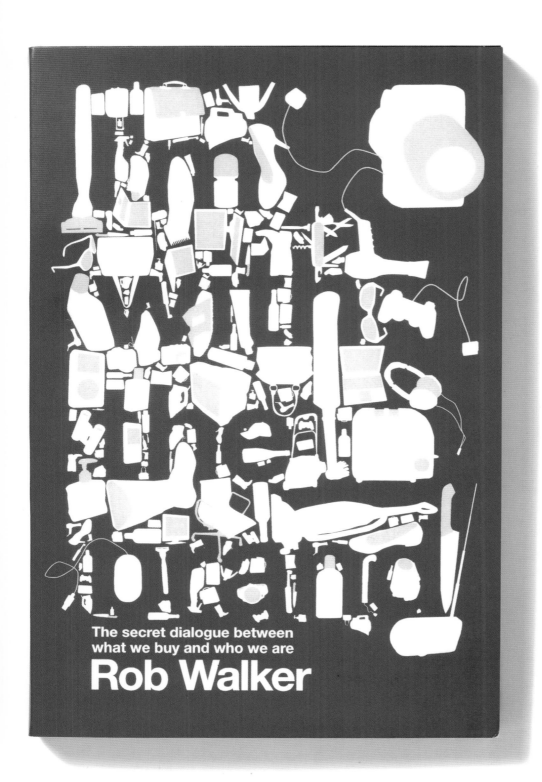

I'm With the Brand

The secret dialogue between
what we buy and who we are

Rob Walker

◄···
Title: **I'm With the Brand**
Medium: **Book cover**
Credits and Rationale:
**Book publishers Constable
and Robinson commissioned
Jawa and Midwich to produce a
"singular" illustration image for
the cover of their new book "I'm
With the Brand" by Rob Walker.
Turning this idea on its head
we produced over 200 singular
images of well known branded
products and arranged these
to create a striking illustrative
typographic cover. We also
produced the typographic
elements for the spine and
reverse of the book.**

...▸

Title: **Mammals of the British Isles**
Medium: **A2 poster**
Credits and Rationale:

**This promotional A2 poster
features all the land mammals
of the British Isles in size order.
After researching the subject
matter we collated our findings
and proceeded to hand illustrate
each animal to be used. These
were then size-referenced and
placed accordingly. To enhance
the poster we introduced
elements of typography and
information graphics.**

Title: **ZO1**
Medium: **Packaging**
Credits and Rationale:
Jawa and Midwich were commissioned by Beauty. Links to create the logo, branding, and packaging for a new sun care range ZO1. The scientific composition of the product was highlighted in our final logo design. The hexagonal form also conveys light reflection and sun glare. Our colour choices for the brand, orange and grey, also help to convey the two elements of sunshine and science. From this logo we created branding guidelines and product packaging. Finally promotional material and a website were created. This work was rewarded with an award from Wallpaper* Magazine for best new beauty design.

Title: **Be Nice to Books**
Medium: **Canvas bag**
Credits and Rationale:
Taking on board a brief from book publishers Pan Macmillan for a 'hand drawn' theme for their canvas book bags. We photographed and researched model poses and objects around a set of quotes supplied by the client. From these we drew illustrations with pencil and finally added hand drawn typographic elements to finalize the design. The bag was screen printed in black and blue onto canvas.

Title: **Young Persons Theatre (YPT)**
Medium: **Foldout poster/ brochure**
Credits and Rationale:
Battersea Arts Centre commissioned Jawa and Midwich to produce a combined poster and leaflet. Utilizing folds one side of the item forms a leaflet whilst the other folds out into poster format. The artwork consists of illustration work created from photographs and typography that was hand drawn and illustrated.

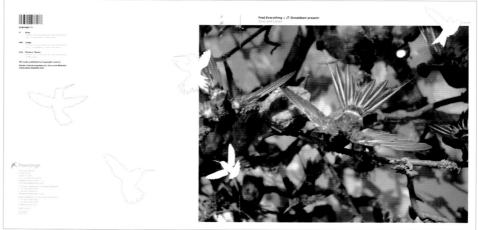

···▸

Title: **Stop and listen**
Medium: **12" Record Sleeve**
Credits and Rationale:
Our art direction for the 'Stop and Listen' sleeve combines elements of illustration and photography. The photograph was taken of an old Victorian bird cabinet filled with a variety of brightly colored humming birds. On top of the photograph we placed some illustrated humming bird shapes.

GREIG ANDERSON

<u>Can you please briefly tell us when and how you started "crossover" design? Also how "crossover" design impacted your design style and beliefs at work?</u>

I never started working with crossover design at a particular point. I have always had various thoughts and ideas for little self-initiated projects, but I never started these projects with the intention of creating a product or trying to make money. They are more about simply realizing little thoughts and ideas that I had always had. Creating my own website became a place to showcase and house these little projects and really it was just about getting them up there and out in front of people to see and to get feed back. I suppose the fascination with button badges came around after I received a button press as a present and I started to enjoy the challenge of working within a 25mm diameter canvas. I instantly loved that it requires no explanation or rationale and literally anything goes, a very different type of working method to my client-based work. I also enjoy the opportunity to package badges in different ways and in some cases, for example, the cassette badges, it is the way that they are packaged that really creates the interest. The badges themselves, although interesting, are not responsible for the overall look of the sets. The fact that they are housed together in a cassette box creates the overall interest and effect.

<u>What is your view of the current trend of "crossover" design? For example, will the emergence of "crossover" design make the current separation of work boundaries fuzzy? Why? Will "crossover" affect the professionalism of design work?</u>

I think that it already has but not adversely, I feel that more and more these days you see designers creating their own self-initiated briefs or projects. Things like the much publicized Made in Bunch project, where an identity system was created by various designers through the art of free submission or response, this shows that things have changed in design and the way that it is applied. We all still do client work, but more and more designers are realizing the benefits of self-exploration and setting themselves briefs. It's a very free place to be, the typical constraints of client work are no longer there and it's a liberating experience for a designer. The real advantage now is that with the use of the internet and more and more blogs, these once never-to-be-seen self-initiated projects are simply with a click of a mouse available to the design masses and more often these days the work that designers and agencies are remembered for is not client work but something where they have cut free and created something just for fun.

Name: Greig Anderson
Company: Effektive
Country: Australia
Email: greig@effektivedesign.co.uk
Website: www.effektivedesign.co.uk

Bio:
Since graduating with an Honours Degree in Applied Graphic Design just 4 years ago, Greig Anderson has been working for the multidisciplinary agency Curious, based in Glasgow. Curious provided Greig with opportunities to work on a variety of projects for various clients, from small independents to large blue chip companies across a variety of sectors. He also produces various freelance works for clients and self-initiated projects, including button badges, posters, and T-Shirt designs under the name of Effektive, which he set up a little over a year ago. He also finds the time to be a contributor and writer on the design blog FormFiftyFive and has also recently set up his own Effektiveblog. In August 2008 Greig moved to Sydney on a working Visa for 12 months and has been working at a Surry Hills based agency for 4 months.

What is your work plan in the future?

I am currently working in Sydney until the autumn of 2009 when I return to the UK. I have no firm plans yet but there are a few exciting ideas in the pipeline so watch this space. I will also be hoping to open a shop section on my website to make some of the various self-initiated projects shown here available for purchase.

The Compact Cassette, often referred to as audio cassette, cassette tape, or simply cassette, is the most successful magnetic tape sound recording format. It consists of two miniature reels, between which a oxide-coated plastic tape, or magnetic tape, is passed and wound. These reels and attendant parts are held inside a protective plastic shell.

- Although originally intended as a medium for dictation, improvements in fidelity, led it to supplant reel-to-reel tape recording. In most applications. Between the 1970s and early 1990s the cassette was one of the two most common formats for prerecorded music alongside the LP and later the Compact Disc.

effektivedesign.co.uk

Title: **Cassette Badge Series**
Medium: **Button Badge Sets**
Dimension: **25mm badges packed in standard size clear cassette boxes**
Credits and Rationale:

Being a child of the eighties I have fond memories of cassettes and I created these limited edition badge sets as a reminder of this past format. There are 12 different cassette types by some of the mainstream tape manufacturers that I remembered having in my childhood. Each set consists of 6x 25mm button badges which are created as circular crops of the actual cassette artwork. These are attached to a printed cassette back board and sealed in a classic cassette box with a custom inlay card giving a brief history of the cassette format. The badges have been featured in a variety of magazines and books including Computer Arts and the first complete full set of these will be taking part in an exhibition in London in late 2008. I have no purposeful intention to increase my range of products but there is bound to be more added as I continue to think of new ideas for products.

Title: **Gness Music Showreel Pack**

Medium: **Single color showreel pack consisting of 8 Page booklet and DVD holder, Box label design and stationery, DVD label design and 25mm button badges**

Dimension: **A5 Pack and booklet**

Credits and Rationale:

As an independent composer it was important that Graham Ness asked me to design an identity, stationery and a showreel that he could send out when pitching for new work. He is a musician who writes music for award-winning, Bafta-nominated TV programs and films and wanted to present himself in such a way. I created a bespoke box design with custom labels, an A5 booklet which showcased his previous work as well as housing a current music CD and full stationery. The design was kept simple and strong as the music was the important factor, but by using black on white and strong use of type throughout it allowed clear and confident messages to be made to prospective clients as well as providing a bit of clarity and standout in what is a highly competitive industry.

CD SHOWREEL

PLEASE TAKE THE TIME TO LISTEN TO MY CURRENT
SHOWREEL CD. IF YOU WOULD LIKE TO RECEIVE
SAMPLES OF A PARTICULAR GENRE OF MUSIC THEN
CONTACT ME WITH YOUR REQUEST.

Title: **Spirograph**
Medium: **Poster and button badge sets**
Dimension: **A2 Posters printed on trace, 25mm button badge sets**
Credits and Rationale:

Inspired by a favourite toy of my childhood, the Spirograph. I decided to create a range of posters in a similar style using today's modern computer technology. The Spirograph produced hand drawn mathematical curves of the variety technically known as hypotrochoids and epitrochoids. I wanted to explore the possibilities of creating something similar using modern design software and by using various techniques in Illustrator I created this set of 6 posters each with their own Spirograph style pattern and a selection of 25mm Button badges which we've packaged in sets of 4 for sale.

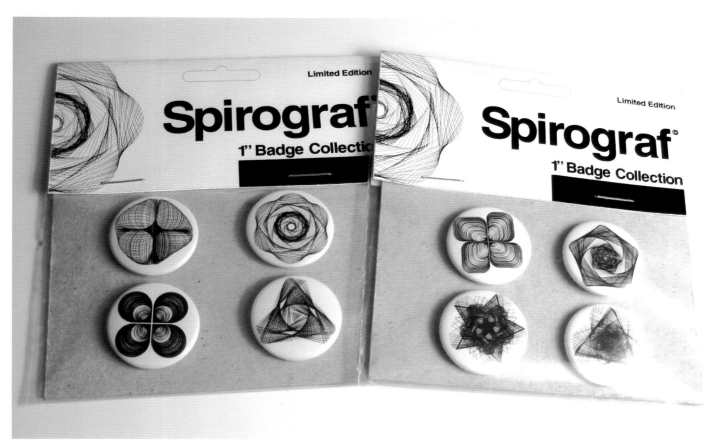

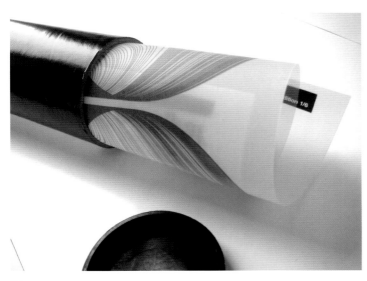

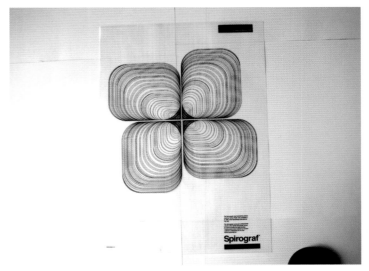

<... :

Title: **Spirograph**

Medium: **Poster and button badge sets**

Dimension: **A2 Posters printed on trace, 25mm button badge sets**

Credits and Rationale:

**Inspired by a favourite toy of my childhood, the Spirograph. I decided to create a range of posters in
a similar style using today's modern computer technology. The Spirograph produced hand drawn
mathematical curves of the variety technically known as hypotrochoids and epitrochoids. I wanted to
explore the possibilities of creating something similar using modern design software and by using various
techniques in Illustrator I created this set of 6 posters each with their own Spirograph style pattern and a
selection of 25mm Button badges which we've packaged in sets of 4 for sale.**

2ERPACK

Can you please briefly tell us when and how you started "crossover" design? Also how "crossover" design impacted your design style and beliefs at work?

Behruz:
My head is always "crossed over," so it's unavoidable that my brain naturally influences my style. My work tries to put this assorted information on point or in a frame.

Hannes:
I started to play with letters, colors, and structures around the age of 15, when I started to write graffiti. I studied the alphabet for years, before even thinking about being a graphic designer. That input has influenced me in my whole career as a graphic designer. The other way around, graphic design influences my graffiti. I can't really separate these two things and that is my personal definition of crossover design.

What is your view of the current trend of "crossover" design? For example, will the emergence of "crossover" design make the current separation of work boundaries fuzzy? Why? Will "crossover" affect the professionalism of design work?

Behruz:
I think "crossover" design is the source for the different design branches. Delivering uncommon realizations and trends. Showing strong character with a variety of different expressions. For me with "crossover" design we have the chance to work hand in hand, influencing society and creating screaming visuals with the reward of acceptance and often "no budget-jobs."

Hannes:
I don't think that "crossover" design is a trend. It is just expanding in different and new directions, which makes the design world even more interesting. On the other hand, a lot of people are trying to be all things to all men, that doesn't create experts that produce high quality work. I still love to work with experts, and combine different skills to make the best output possible.

What is your work plan in the future?

Behruz:
No straight plans!! Instant decisions, please!!
Hannes:
To stay happy!

Name: Hannes Mussbach & BehruzTschaitschian
Company: 2erpack
Country: Germany
Email: info@2erpack.com
Web: www.2erpack.com

Bios:
Behruz Tschaitschian:
Age 31, studied in Hamburg and gained my degree in 2000 in Communication Design. I started working during the big internet boom of 1998, creating websites, working for one of the first Internet streaming radio stations in Germany. After the Internet crash, I regenerated myself in to doing more design based works, working for agencies like Mutabor and Ligalux. Besides getting to know other countries in 2007, I decided to work as a freelancer in a company with Hannes Mussbach, as 2erpack. Additionally I am also working as a tutor at the Institute of Design in Hamburg.
Hannes Mussbach:
Age 28, when I was 15 years old I started to draw graffiti, which was the basis for my interest in graphic design. I studied in Hamburg and graduated in 2004 in communication design. During my studies I started an internship at Ligalux, a corporate design agency. After getting my diploma, I continued my career at Ligalux and worked there till January 2008 as an Art Director. In my free time, I always supported free non-budget projects, where I could combine all my skills. In January Behruz and I decided to work together as a freelance team, like in the old Ligalux days. On the weekends (yeah, we still have something like that!) I still go out with my graffiti crew (www.chosenfewcrew.de) to paint murals on the weekend.

····▸
Title: **Vector**
Credits and Rationale:
One of our passions, creating, types, logos, and various illustrations.

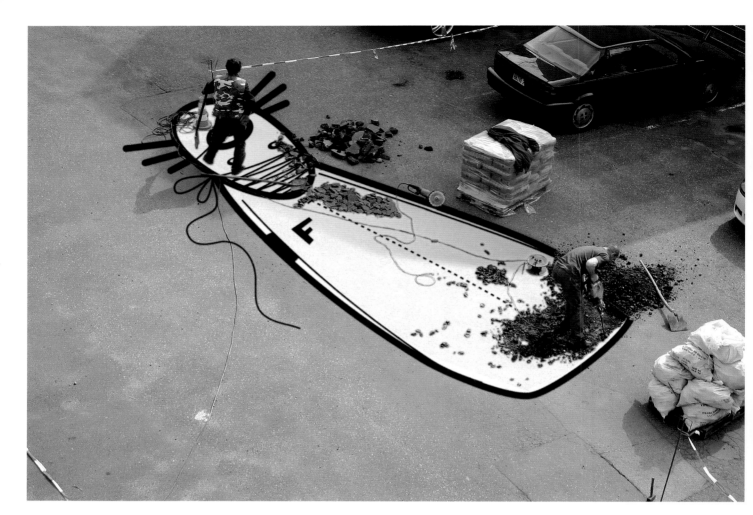

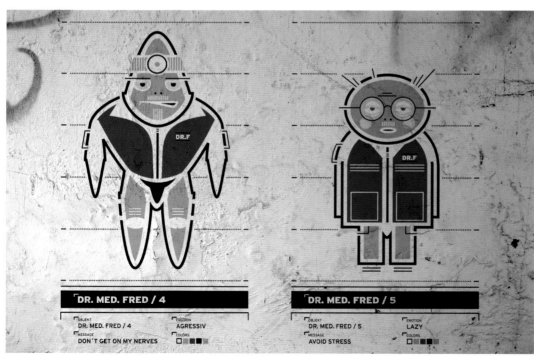

DR. MED. FRED / 4

┌ OBJEKT
DR. MED. FRED / 4

┌ EMOTION
AGGRESSIV

┌ MESSAGE
DON'T GET ON MY NERVES

┌ COLORS

DR. MED. FRED / 5

┌ OBJEKT
DR. MED. FRED / 5

┌ EMOTION
LAZY

┌ MESSAGE
AVOID STRESS

┌ COLORS

Title: **Vector**
Credits and Rationale:
**One of our passions, creating,
types, logos, and various
illustrations.**

Title: **Graffiti**
Credits and Rationale:
www.chosenfewcrew.de

↕ ⋯→

Title: **Blockparty Entertainment**
Medium: **Flyer, Poster, handi-crafted ghettoblasters**
Rationale:
Blockparty Entertainment has been a party institution in Hamburg since 2002, influenced and always playing Old School Rap, Miami Bass, Geddo-Tech, New Jack Swing, HipHouse, Heavy Metal Rap, Early Dancehall.
Credits: **E-Z IRON CEE, Stoecker Stereo**

DRAMAKING
ONE STEP
AWAY FRO
LEAVING
BEHIND
OM
YOU
ONE
DRUGS OR ME
TWO
WASTING MY HONESTY
THREE
ON TIME
FOUR
GOODNIGHT
©2008 DRAMAKING PRODUCTIONS
WRITTEN AND PRODUCED BY DRAMAKING
CONTACT: MAIL@DRAMA-KING.COM
CHECK OUT WWW.DRAMA-KING.COM
DESIGN BY 2ERPACK

DRAMAKING

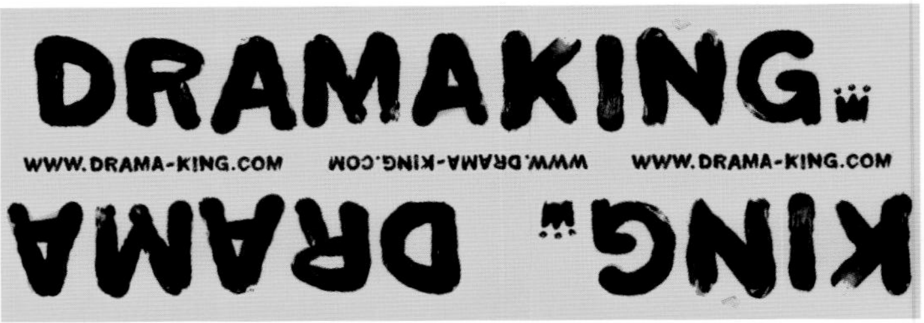
DRAMAKING
WWW.DRAMA-KING.COM
WWW.DRAMA-KING.COM
WWW.DRAMA-KING.COM
KING DRAMA

Title: **DRAMAKING**
Medium: **Logo, CD Artwork, sticker**
Rationale:
Finger drawn Artwork. No budget design for an upcoming alternative Rockband from Hamburg.
Credits: **www.drama-king.com**

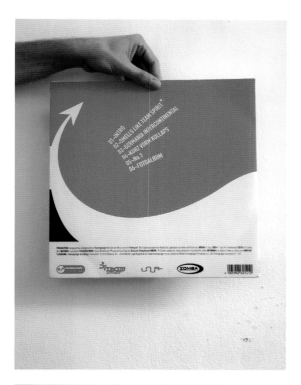

Title: **Teamsport Transporter**
Medium:
Vinyl, Record Cover
Rationale:
Abstract illustration showing the transportation of words underlining the lyrical shape of this German HipHop EP.
Credits: **S-Mode a.k.a Ramin Tschaitschian a.k.a our brother, Dj Franky Nutz, Bruder Garl, Stoecker Stereo, Trainingslager Recordings.**

Title: **Berryfamily character design**
Medium: **T-shirts, Banner, Cups, Balloons**
Rationale:
We wanted to create an uncommon corporate design for a kindergarten in Germany. We resisted designing a logo. Children want to play, so we decided to coin those droll characters.
Credits: **Ligalux, HYPERLINK "http://www.ligalux.de"**

berryfamily

BRIGITTE   DAS DOPPELTE THOMAS   HERMANN   SIGGI   KARSTEN   ROSWITHA   PETER

GUNNAR   HARTMUT   HARALD   KLAUS   ALFONS   WOLFGANG   ZORAK

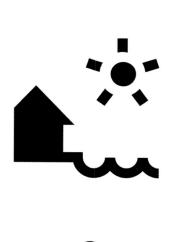

Title: **Interhome Icons**
Medium: **Diverse**
Rationale:
It was a challenge in creating these tiny icons for a Swiss holiday provider on a 4 x 4 mm area of information.
Credits: **This work was created for Palisander Werbung & Design GbR.**

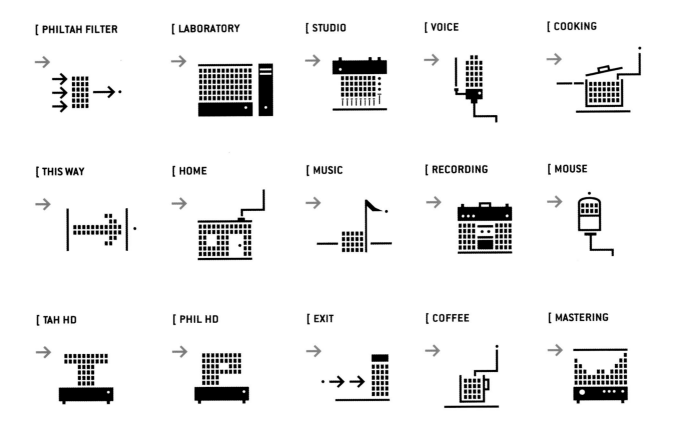

[PHILTAH FILTER

[LABORATORY

[STUDIO

[VOICE

[COOKING

[THIS WAY

[HOME

[MUSIC

[RECORDING

[MOUSE

[TAH HD

[PHIL HD

[EXIT

[COFFEE

[MASTERING

Title: **Dontplaywithmyyoyo**
Medium: **YoYo's**
Rationale:
Partyseries in Hamburg. We tried to introduce a different form of handout, imprinting a yoyo, celebrating the good old times.
Credits:
Buzz-T, Stoecker Stereo, Foto: copywright Yvonne Amankwa Photography.

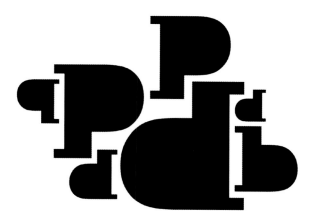

piano movers

piano movers

piano movers
Klavier-, Tresor- und
Flügeltransporte

↕ ⋯→
Title: **Piano Movers Corporate Design**
Medium: **Stationary, Logo, Key visual**
Credits and Rationale:
Corporate Design for a small enterprise specialized in moving pianos.

→ PRODUCTIONS

Title: **PHILTAH Productions**
Medium: **Logo, Icons, Poster, Rings, Exhibition**
Credits and Rationale:
Olivier Karnapp, Phillip Falk, Butze

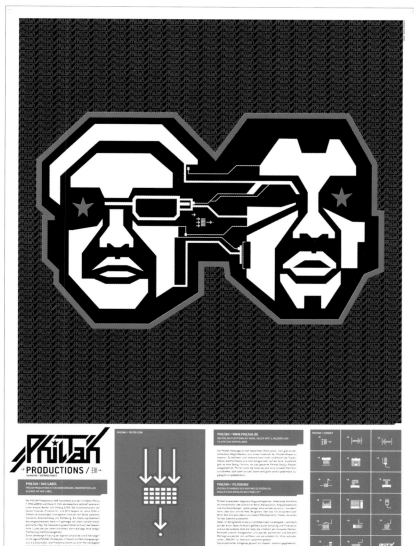

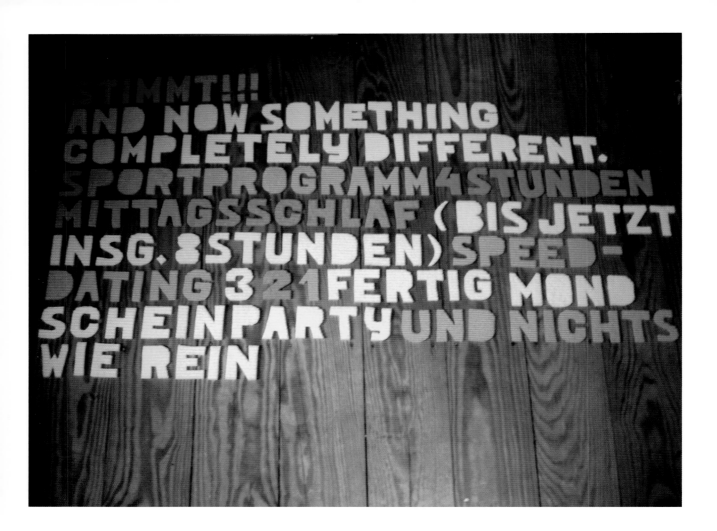

STIMMT!!!
AND NOW SOMETHING
COMPLETELY DIFFERENT.
SPORTPROGRAMM 4 STUNDEN
MITTAGSSCHLAF (BIS JETZT
INSG. 8 STUNDEN) SPEED-
DATING 3 2 1 FERTIG MOND
SCHEINPARTY UND NICHTS
WIE REIN

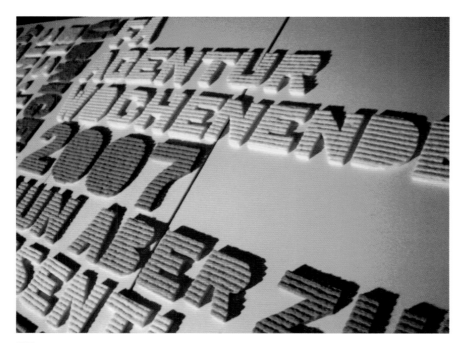

◄··· ⁝
Title: **Spongetype**
Medium: **Sponge**
Credits and Rationale:
**Type Experiment with different
Materials. One of them is a
riffled sponge used for washing
dishes. Good to hand-cut.**

↥ ⋯→

Title: **Flyer**

Credits and Rationale:

**A mix of Flyers created over
the past five years for different
events.**

↕ ⋯→
Title: **Flyer**
Credits and Rationale:
A mix of Flyers created over
the past five years for different
events.

108

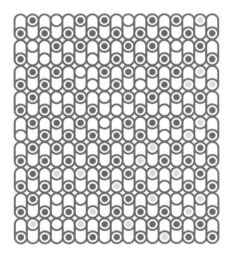

original jazz club

IMMER DER 2. DIENSTAG IM MONAT

concerts & dj-sessions

immer Luna | Bergstr. 17a | Kiel
Einlass 20.00h | Beginn 21.00h

Subsonic Pressure - Finest Drum n Bass

SUBZ MATIK PAT
MC UPPER CUT

Special Guest

KABUKI

Frankfurt - Precision Breakbeat Research
Combination Rec. Liquid V

FR 27 01 06 23h
LUNA CLUB KIEL
BERGSTRASSE 17A

3Y SP

Subsonic Pressure

original jazz club

IMMER DER 2. DIENSTAG IM MONAT

concerts & dj-sessions

immer Luna | Bergstr. 17a | Kiel
Einlass 20.00h | Beginn 21.00h

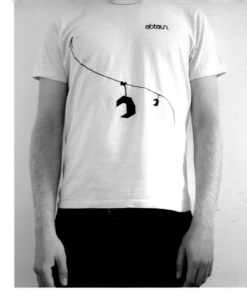

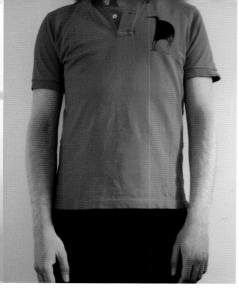

Title: **Shirts**
Medium: **Textile**
Credits and Rationale:
What we wear.

BENNY LUK

Can you please briefly tell us when and how you started "crossover" design? Also how "crossover" design impacted your design style and beliefs at work?

My first "crossover" design was in 2004. I worked with Sony X Levis, called "Simply Life." I had my first chance to express my style with commercial design. I gained new inspiration and direction through the creation of the project.

What is your view of the current trend of "crossover" design? For example, will the emergence of "crossover" design make the current separation of work boundaries fuzzy? Why? Will "crossover" affect the professionalism of design work?

It's refreshing to have this type of relationship between designers and clients. It doesn't change the principle concept of design. There is a difference between commercial work and "crossover" work. It's nice to have the freedom to influence the "crossover" design with my own input; whereas there are more restrictions with commercial work.

What is your work plan in the future?

I wish to develop different types of work with new clients.

Name: Benny Luk
Company: Sixstation
Country: Hong Kong, China
Email: benny@sixstation.com
Website: www.sixstation.com

Bio:
Benny Luk, 28 years old. A graphic, web, font designer, and illustrator. Sixstation was first started as a personal experimental website in 2000. From 2004 to present it changed into a SOHO. He mainly works with international clients such as Nike Asia, MTV Asia, and Sony X Levis etc. Sixstation's main design style is mixed with modern contemporary and rich traditional Asian culture. In recent years Sixstation has received many local and international awards.
Awards include in 06, 07, 08 Tokyo Type Directors Club excellence award, 02/05 Hong Kong Designers Association Awards Silver, Bronze and excellence awards, Winner of
Favourite Website Award 03. He has numerous design magazine interviews about his work, including Japan + 81, UK Computerarts, Korea Web Design , and Taiwan Xfun.

···›
Title: **Computer arts**
Credits and Rationale:
Cover illustration for UK creative magazine.

Title: **Computer arts**
Credits and Rationale:
Cover illustration for UK creative magazine.

...▸

Title: **Readymade Magazine (RMM)**
Credits and Rationale:
Artistic illustration for Adobe Creative gallery. The artwork is shown in local creator's lifestyle magazine.

ZEN
GARDEN

115

‹··· ↑
Title: **Fayte**
Credits and Rationale:
Fayte is about the exploration of relationships with the world and our lives through our exquisite merchandise.

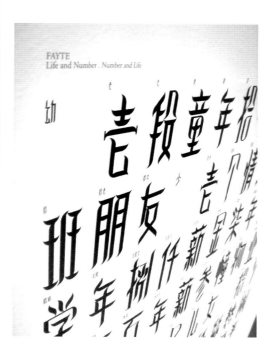

FAYTE
Life and Number . Number and Life

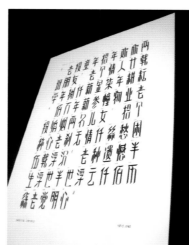

Title: **Fayte poster**
Credits and Rationale: **Fayte**
is about the exploration of
relationship with the world and
our lives through our exquisite
merchandise.

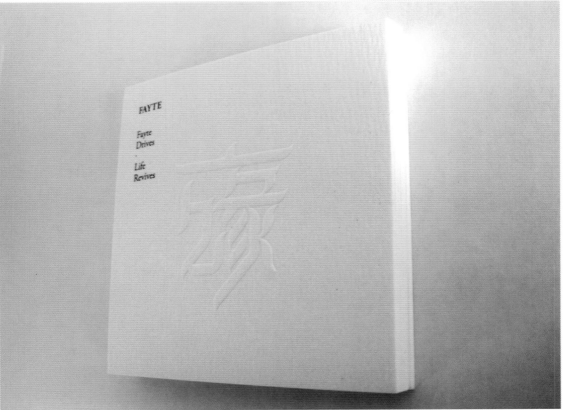

←···

Title: **Fayte name card**
Credits and Rationale:
**Fayte is about the exploration of
relationship with the world and
our lives through our exquisite
merchandise.**

Title: **World without strangers**
Credits and Rationale:
**T-shirt design for the Giordano
artist collaboration project
"World without strangers."**

Title: **Manjianghong Poster**
Credits and Rationale:
An experimental artwork that combines the traditional poem Manjianghong with modern typography.

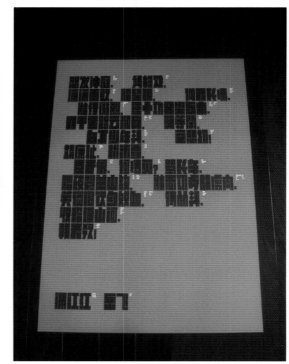

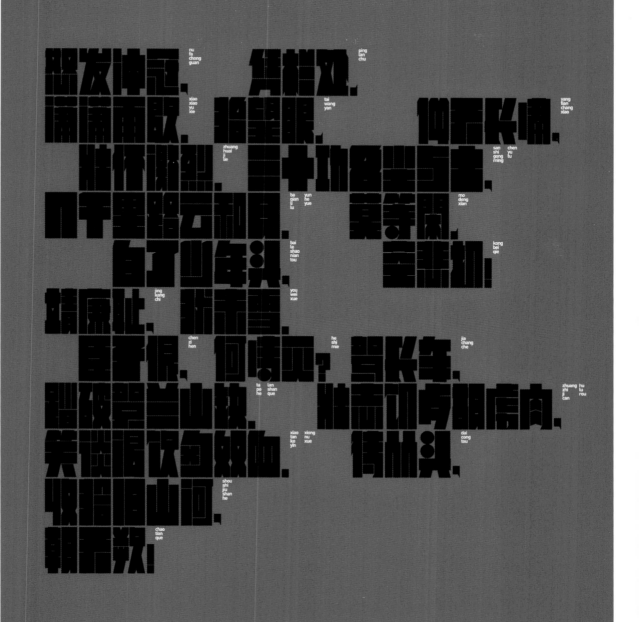

‹··· ↕

Title: **Nikebasketball**

Credits and Rationale:

Artwork for the new Nike basketball campaign [My game is made outside!!]. In this project sixstation was invited to work with the basketball player Jason Kidd.

DUDU TORRES

G M W

Can you please briefly tell us when and how you started "crossover" design? Also how "crossover" design impacted your design style and beliefs at work?

Since high school, I have always been connected to the communication area. I became interested in anything connected to it. And this continued with my entry into college. All areas interested me. I started with advertising, and went through to graphic design. In the meantime, I became interested in fashion and had a brand called Ventura, which was later discontinued. I became interested in video (which led me to do a course in After Effects), but today I focus on graphic design, working mostly with branding, events and mobile design. In 2008, I attended a course in Flash to start developing for the web. I am a lover of all areas of design and enjoy participating in everything possible, to become, increasingly, a complete designer. Photography is a hobby of mine and, someday, I wish to return to working in fashion.

What is your view of the current trend of "crossover" design? For example, will the emergence of "crossover" design make the current separation of work boundaries fuzzy? Why? Will "crossover" affect the professionalism of design work?

I believe that the exchange of experiences gained in the implementation of projects in different areas will only add quality to every designer. Being complete, the designer acquires a broader and decisive vision on all projects in which he/she participates. This change in the quality of professionals directly affects the level of work, which, consequently, will lead the market to a whole new level of professionalism.

What is your work plan in the future?

Currently, my plans are to continue producing and creating new solutions for the projects that I work on. As I said above, one day I wish to return to fashion, in addition to working, even temporarily, in a foreign agency.

Name: Dudu Torres
Country: Brazil
Email: dudutorres@me.com
dudutorres@dudutorres.com
Website: www.dudutorres.com

Bio:
Hi! I am a 25 year old Brazilian designer, impassioned by Design in its various forms. I am an impulsive man, crazy about references, and I always like to upgrade and learn new ways to develop my work. I'm currently working as a designer in a communication agency called Conception, and like most of us, developing projects as a freelancer. Photography is a great hobby of mine, I have developed many projects recently.

⇕ ⇕
Title: **A vellar Torres**

Medium: **Branding**

Credits and Rationale:

For a Law Firm

⇕
Title: **Insight! Arquitetura**

Medium: **Branding**

Credits and Rationale:

Designers: Dudu Torres and Bruno Couto

PRODUCTS **TIM**
Icon for the special offers and services TIM.

TIM WEB CALLER
Software used to connect TIM WEB from a Mac or PC.

TIM WEB BROADBAND
Broadband wireless internet.

TIM WEB BROADBAND
Broadband wireless internet.

Title: **Products TIM Icon**
Medium: **Illustration Design**
Dimension: **420 x 250 mm**

Title: **TIM Web Caller Icon**
Medium: **Illustration Design**
Graphic Design
Dimension: **420 x 250 mm**

Title: **IM Web Icon**
Medium: **Illustration Design**
Graphic Design
Dimension: **420 x 250 mm**

HUAWEI ICONS
Icons used in all TIM Huawei mobile phones.

TIM THEMES
Wallpapers used on TIM mobile phones.

TIM TV
Interface for the TIM mobile TV.

Title: **Huawei Icons**

Medium: **Illustration Design /Graphic Design / Mobile Design**

Credits and Rationale:

Icons developed for all TIM Brazil / Huawei mobile phones.

Title: **TIM Themes**

Medium: **Illustration Design / Graphic Design / Mobile Design**

Credits and Rationale:

Themes created for TIM Brazil mobile phones.

Title: **TIM TV**

Medium: **Graphic Design / Mobile Design**

Credits and Rationale:

Interface created for the application TIM TV.

129

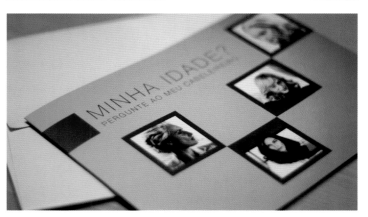

Title: **L'Orèal Catalog**
Medium: **Graphic Design**
Credits and Rationale:
Designer: Dudu Torres

Title: **L'Orèal Folder**
Medium: **Graphic Design**
Credits and Rationale:
Designer: Dudu Torres

...▸

Title: **Tatame Magazine**
Medium: **Graphic Design, Editorial Design**
Credits and Rationale:
Magazine cover developed for Tatame
Designers: Dudu Torres and Paulo Amendoeira

⋮

Title: **Eletrobras 2004 Annual Report**
Medium: **Editorial Design / Graphic Design**
Dimension: **420 x 250 mm**
Credits and Rationale:
Designers: Dudu Torres and Paulo Amendoeira

Title: **Project Whales**
Medium: **Branding / Web Design**
Dimension: **420 x 250 mm**
Credits and Rationale:
Designer: Dudu Torres

Title: **Ruta**
Medium: **Branding /**
Graphic Design
Dimension: **420 x 250 mm**
Credits and Rationale: **Visual**
Identity for a "Harley focused"
company (restaurant, mechanic,
insurance). Designers: Dudu
Torres and Andre Vianna

Title: **Dudu Torres**
Medium: **Branding /**
Graphic Design
Dimension: **420 x 250 mm**
Credits and Rationale:
Designer: Dudu Torres

...→

Title: **Ventura**
Medium: **Branding**
Dimension: **420 x 250 mm**
Credits and Rationale:
Fashion Brand
Designer: **Dudu Torres**

...→ ⋮

Title: **Ruta Cuzco**
Medium: **Illustration Design /
Graphic Design**
Dimension: **420 x 250 mm**
Credits and Rationale:
**T-Shirt Illustration created for a
Cuzco Road Trip**
Designer: **Dudu Torres**

Title: **Ruta Bathroom Doors**
Medium: **Graphic Design**
Credits and Rationale:
Designers: Dudu Torres and André Vianna
Photographer: Bruno Ryfer

...▸

Title: **Cinema Music Festival**
Medium: **Graphic Design**
Credits and Rationale:
Designer: Dudu Martins
Photographer: Dudu Torres

O ENCONTRO DO CINEMA COM A MÚSICA EM UM GRANDE CENÁRIO.

2º FESTIVAL
CINE
MÚSICA

CONSERVATÓRIA 2008 - 4 A 7 DE SETEMBRO

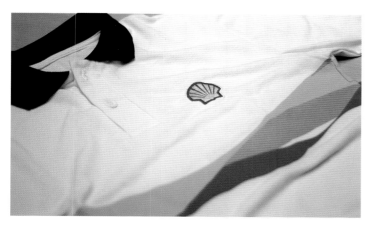

◄...

Title: **Shell Uniform**
Medium: **Fashion Design /**
Graphic Design
Dimension: **420 x 250 mm**
Credits and Rationale:
Uniform created to be used on
all Shell Events.
Designer: Dudu Torres

⋮

Title: **Shell HSSE Forum 2008**
Medium: **Graphic Design**
Dimension: **420 x 250 mm, Vector**
Credits and Rationale:
Designer: Dudu Torres

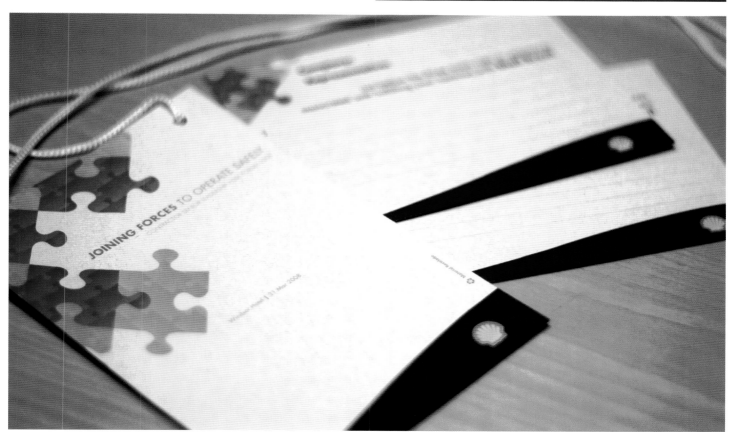

IDEA OSHIMA

Can you please briefly tell us when and how you started "crossover" design? Also how "crossover" design impacted your design style and beliefs at work?

I see myself just working in graphic design as other Japanese designers do, and I don't think of COD (crossover design) as a particular feature of my work. When I choose photographers and illustrators for my projects, however, I may be thinking about a collaborative effect over different disciplines.

What is your view of the current trend of "crossover" design? For example,will the emergence of "crossover" design make the current separation of work boundaries fuzzy? Why? Will "crossover" affect the professionalism of design work?

I don't consider COD a recent trend. I think design itself has contained aspects of crossover from the beginning. Maybe the classification of design that emerged in modernistic thinking created borders in design. I think that the borders in design must have been ambiguous.

What is your work plan in the future?

Go on design. I don't create works for my own purpose: I get commissions and I react to them. However I do hope that being included in an overseas book like this one would bring me opportunities to widen my scope and activities. For me communicating with people overseas is itself quite a crossover phenomenon.

Name: Idea Oshima
Country: Japan
Email: idea@t3.rim.or.jp

Bio:
Born in Tochigi, 1968. Graduated from Tokyo Zokei University in 1991. After studying film making he became a graphic designer on self-employed basis mainly for films and art museum exhibitions, along with designs for fashion catalogues and book editorials etc.

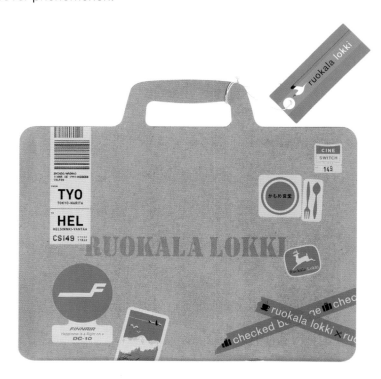

Title: **Kamome Shokudo**
Medium: **Cardboard paper, Uncoated pape**
Dimension: **182 × 257 mm**
Copyright: ©**Photo: Yoko Takahashi c**
2006 "Kamome" Company

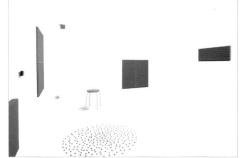

Title: **A Notebook Unwritten**
Medium: **Cardboard paper**
Dimension: **182 × 257 mm**
Copyright: **©Mitsuhiro Yamagiwa**
KOKUYO Co., Ltd. All rights reserved.

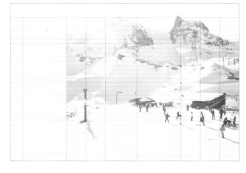

Title: **BEAUTIFUL NEW WORLD
Contemporary Visual Culture
from Japan**
Medium: **Cardboard paper, Mirror
paper, Uncoated paper**
Dimension: **230 × 257 mm**

···→

Title: **Conversation with Art, On
Art**
Medium: **Uncoated paper**
Dimension: **210 × 297 mm**
Copyright: **©Tokyo Opera City Art
Gallery**

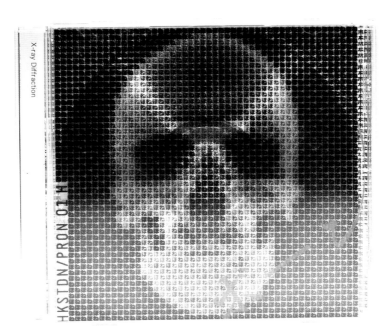

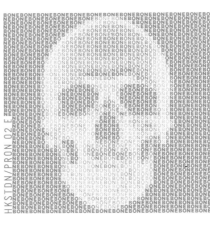

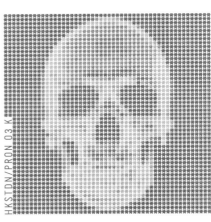

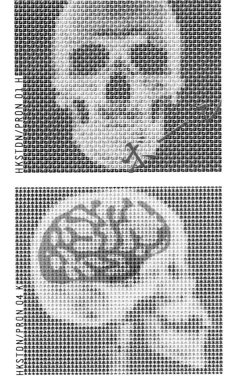

Title: **Bone**
Medium: **Clear film, Plastic, Compact disc**
Dimension: **141 × 123 mm**
Copyright: © **Photo Mitsuru Hirota**

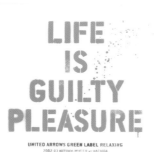

Title: **LIFE IS GUILTY PLEASURE**
United Arrows Green Label Relaxing
2002-2003 Autumn-Winter
Medium: **Uncoated paper**
Dimension: **163 × 163 mm**

Title: **Style for Living**
Medium: **Cardboard paper, Clear vinyl**
Dimension: **154 × 154 mm**

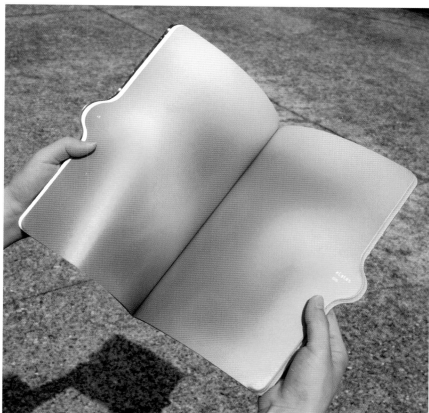

Title: **Space-Jack!**
Medium: **Mirror paper, Uncoated paper, Antique paper**
Dimension: **182 × 257 mm**

QIANG HAN

Can you please briefly tell us when and how you started "crossover" design? Also how "crossover" design impacted your design style and beliefs at work?

I felt that the reality of life required me to pursue a road in design where I create everything from scratch; much like a caveman does in his village. This type of "crossover" design allows one to be active in passiveness, and vice versa. It is very much a natural part of life. I try to experiment to allow unseen designs to manifest themselves during this fleeting life, but without compromising my personal themes of light, energy, love, interest, relaxation, and socialization. With the arrangement of image clips in my heart, I try to bring to people relaxation, convenience, and comfort.

What is your view of the current trend of "crossover" design? For example, will the emergence of "crossover" design make the current separation of work boundaries fuzzy? Why? Will "crossover" affect the professionalism of design work?

I don't know, and do not care much about the "crossover" trend. I think this lies within personal needs, and since I haven't even begun to understand my personal needs, I don't care about it much, haha. If it should be done, then do it. The ability to naturally not perform is not easy. For me, there never was anything called "professionalism," and I am always changing. Design is in the expression of self, so the means should be free, the attitude apparent. Living on this earth, there is no other way, I think, than to mimic nature, if one was to maximize comfort.

What is your work plan in the future?

Play hard, with the friends who love me; earn money! Just joking, if you're lucky, generate some fame, and everything becomes easier. Dream every day, climb a ladder once in a while, jump when you're happy, and smile when you're troubled.

Name: Qiang Han
Country: China
Email: designer010@yahoo.cn

Bio:
2002   Revamped part of the temple door at the end of the year at Guangfuguan Taoist Temple .
2003   Interior design for bars around Beijing's Lotus market. Manager and designer for a wicker furniture store in the same area. Participated in many of Beijing's electronic parties. Started to co-operate with a few of Beijing's electronic music labels: China PumpFactory, Exectro Beijing, Funky Groove, anddécor for parties (to date).
2004   With the ending of the SARS epidemic and with some serious consideration, I sold all my bars and shops and began to focus on interior design work, developing furniture and décor pieces. Also began self-learning construction basics.
2005 – 2006   After touring Europe began independently designing Henry Lee's third Beijing club, Ruifu Social Lounge Club. My work included the complete special design of the second floor, and furniture. The finished work was nominated for the 2005 American Interior Design Hall of Fame.
2006 – 2007   Designed bars and restaurants for friends'.
2007 – 2008   Designed the Minimal Lounge Boutique Hotel while on vacation at Yunnan. Began designing the D+Y film salon in Beijing.

...›
Title: **D+Y film salon**
Years: **2007.08.-2008.08.**
Credits and Rationale:
Project at Daxiangfeng Hutong No. 11 yard, Houhai, Beijing. The wind makes up the walls, clouds the roof, water the earth… I was quite split when doing this, going crazy a few times. But I did end up finding my door. Enough talk, please observe.

...▸

Title: **Minimal Lounge Boutique Hotel**

Years: **2007.05-2007.10.**

Credits and Rationale:

This hotel is at Guangbi Alley No. 77, Zhongyi Street, Dayan old town, Lijiang, Yunnan Province. My situation was rather unstable at the time; I wanted lots, but achieved little. Really, I just loved Yunnan and Lijiang. Minimal Lounge Boutique Hotel is the "cloud" of Yunnan as per my inspiration. Every room is a piece of cloud, allowing comfort, and a feeling of being loved by everyone.

Title: **Minimal Lounge Boutique Hotel**

Years: **2007.05-2007.10.**

Credits and Rationale:

This hotel is at Guangbi Alley No. 77, Zhongyi Street, Dayan old town, Lijiang, Yunnan Province. My situation was rather unstable at the time; I wanted lots, but achieved little. Really, I just loved Yunnan and Lijiang. Minimal Lounge Boutique Hotel is the "cloud" of Yunnan as per my inspiration. Every room is a piece of cloud, allowing comfort, and a feeling of being loved by everyone.

KATSUNORI AOKI

Can you please briefly tell us when and how you started "crossover" design? Also how "crossover" design impacted your design style and beliefs at work?

In postwar Japan, there has been a structure of society divided vertically and in that structure; advertising agencies have held power for half a century. For 10 years the media has changed enormously in this digital society and the time has finally come when creators are able to express freely their own ideas or thoughts, I think.

What is your view of the current trend of "crossover" design? For example,will the emergence of "crossover" design make the current separation of work boundaries fuzzy? Why? Will "crossover" affect the professionalism of design work?

From the point of view of direction, there would be no drastic change even if we made posters, movies, or 3D works. I believe that from each point of view, original works would be produced.

What is your work plan in the future?

When we produce something new, it is important to retain the good points of the previous experience. In the current climate, I would like to try to make things clearer, but also something that is bigger and better, including popularity.

Name: Katsunori Aoki
Company: Butterfly Stroke Inc.
Country: Japan
Email: info@btf.co.jp
Web: www.butterfly-stroke.com

Bio:
Katsunori Aoki is an Art director / creative director / graphic designer and President of Butterfly Stroke Inc. Not only does he handle advertising work, he also works on graphics and images. He is an artist who handles everything from the planning stage to the presentation. He uses scribble-like sketches and photos or computer generated graphics with ease. He is well known for his sharp visual creativity, and has many corporate clients. He was born in Kanda, Tokyo on the 9th of May 1965. After having worked at SUN-AD agency, he established Butterfly Stroke Inc. in 1999.

Title: **COPET**
Medium: **Poster, Exhibition, Sculpture, Animation video, Paper kit**

···▸
Title: **COPET**
Medium: **Poster, Exhibition, Sculpture, Animation video, Paper kit**

オリンピックを福岡・九州へ

Capek. exhibition in FUKUOKA　2006.06.08(thu)～07.03(mon) 11:00～20:00　abc gallery

Title: **COPET**
Medium: **Poster, Exhibition,
Sculpture, Animation video,
Paper kit**

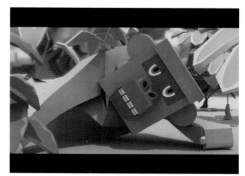

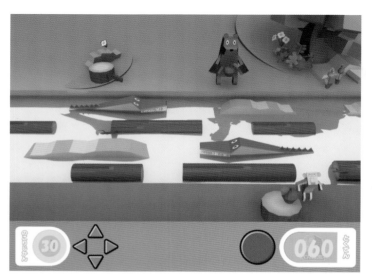

Title: **Coca-Cola summer campaign "kuma cool summer"**
Medium: **Poster, TVCM, Novelty goods (TV, Desk fan, speaker with iPod keyholder, Figure, etc)**

PACHINCO HALL DESIGN COMPETITION

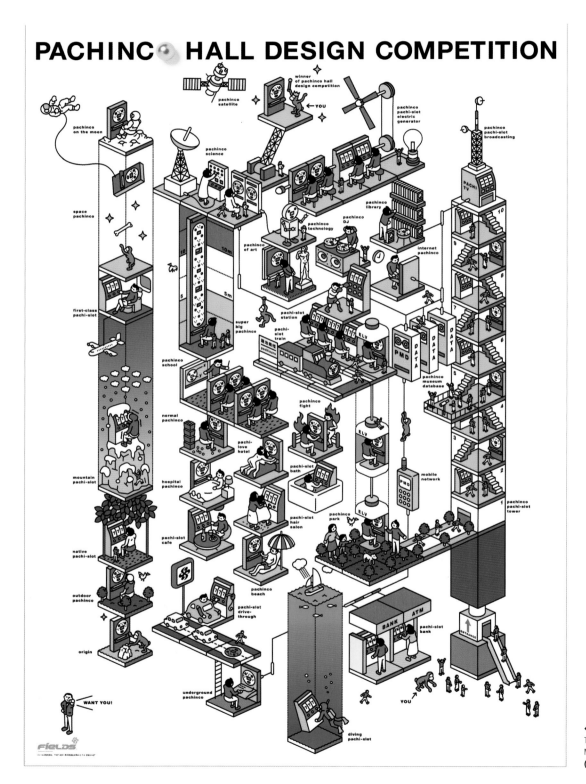

Title: **Fields**
Medium: **Poster, Goods, Book**
(company guide)

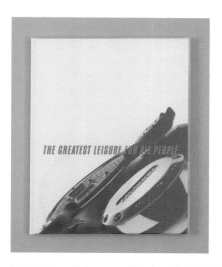

Title: **Fields**
Medium: **Poster, Goods, Book
(company guide)**

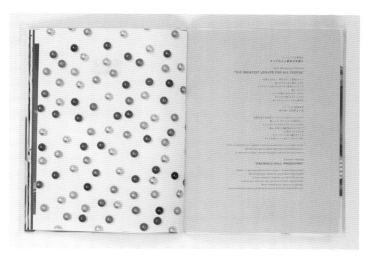

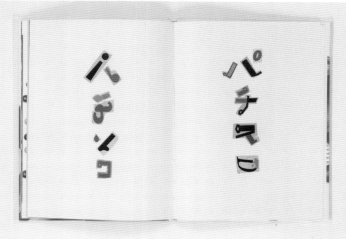

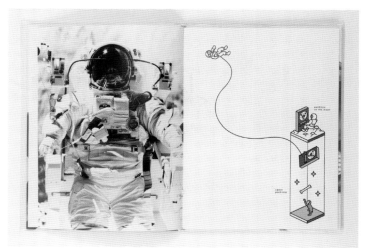

←··· ↕
Title: **Globe2 pop/rock**
Medium: **Poster, CD jacket,
and booklet, T-shirts, Outdoor
advertising**

Title: **Good Design Presentation**
Medium: **Poster, Goods, Book,
Exhibition decoration**

Title: **Tokyo Designer Gakuin College**
Medium: **Poster, School Guidebook, Notebook**

Title: **Hangame**
Medium: **Poster, Sculpture, Novelty goods, Outdoor advertising**

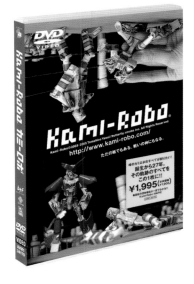

Title: **Kami-Robo**

Medium: **Poster, Video, Goods (Figure, Mask, Paper kit, Book, Visual book, DVD, Card game, Beer, Clothes,)**

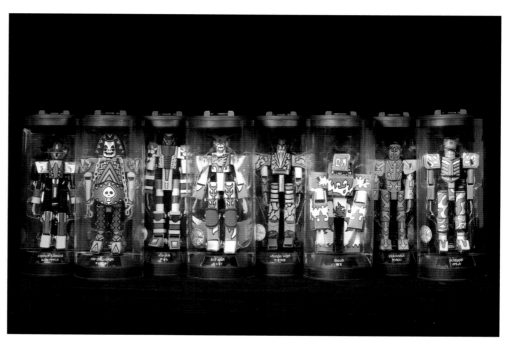

Title: **Seven Samurai**
Medium: **Poster, DVD, Pinball machine**

Title: **Kami-Robo Fight Maoh vs Bluekiller**
Medium: **Poster, Panel, Visual book, Mask, Costume**

TEA TIME STUDIO `G` `W`

Can you please briefly tell us when and how you started "crossover" design? Also how "crossover" design impacted your design style and beliefs at work?

Crossover is a necessary concept for any creative aspect of life, sometimes a complete concept for an identity comes from movie dialog, or a plastic bag, or a nice meal, why not? I find that any job has creative aspects and creativity must be an open door to any influence, and to practice many disciplines take us to places we never expected. Sometimes I find a solution to a graphic design work while I am cooking, or taking photographs.

What is your view of the current trend of "crossover" design? For example, will the emergence of "crossover" design make the current separation of work boundaries fuzzy? Why? Will "crossover" affect the professionalism of design work?

Absolutely, there are two tendencies, specialization (boring and probably not very interesting way to learn more skills) or baroque creative crossover "we can do everything" attitude, I like that, and I find it as a way of work that takes more chances in learning something in the process and creating a fresh approach to other disciplines.

What is your work plan in the future?

Continue working on TTS projects and sharing with other creative as many projects as I can, since I find that learning is the only way to survive in any creative discipline, so I need to contrast my concepts with other people to learn from other point of views.

Name: Sebastian Litmanovich
Company: Tea Time Studio
Country: Spain
Email: ALOHA@teatimestudio.com
Website: www.teatimestudio.com

Bio:
Hello, I am Sebastian Litmanovich, the alma mater and only soul at Tea Time Studio, which is my creative studio for visual, conceptual, & commercial works. I am a very curious person, always trying to learn something from each work experience, as this is the only way to grow and progress. I love to collaborate with other creatives, as TTS is a solo project I need to compare ideas and concepts while learning from other people's points of view. This happens especially with my soul mate Ana, who is the creative director of her studio Alan The Gallant. She is really a total sponge and the most curious person I've ever met, so we really enjoy and learn by sharing our professional experiences as well.

···›
Title: **Audiovisual Documentary "La Danza Sincronizada de los Cacahuetes Magnéticos" (or The Synchronized Dance of the Magnetic Peanuts)**
Medium: **All video & music**
Credits and Rationale:
Graphic design, Script, Direction and realization for the Audiovisual Documentary "La Danza Sincronizada de los Cacahuetes Magnéticos" (or The Synchronized Dance of the Magnetic Peanuts), made with aBe and performed at Sonar 2005. "The Synchronised Dance of the Magnetic Peanuts" is a disturbing documentary made by Alex Beltran and Sebastián Litmanovich. The in-depth investigation discloses important testimonies, including that of Adam West. Revealing experiments place Claude's theory in doubt and even question whether Man did in fact reach the Moon. The audio-visual documentary will be presented live.
See the movie here: **www.cacahuetes.net**

Title: **Federico Aubele's Panamericana, a new albums identity and visual concept**

Medium: **Photo, collage, illustrations, design, etc...**

Dimension: **This particular case was made for a CD digipack and other elements such as T-shirts and a vinyl jacket**

Credits and Rationale:

Identity, photos, art direction & illustration for the album Panamericana and for the solo albums by Federico Aubele, released by ESL Music, USA. The main concept for the album design is based on the Pan-American Highway. This is the longest road in the world that goes from South America to Canada. I had to create a tracing of the map of the road using many maps from every country in which the road appears, then I put them together or meld both concepts, Federico Aubele's shape, (taken from the press photos that I took of him) and the American continent's shape to conceptualize both icons in one main logo for the whole edition of singles and posters.

abcdefghijklmnopqrstuvwxyz
ABCDEFGHIJKLMNOPQRSTUVWXYZ

1234567890!"·$%&/()=¿,'?""÷
ŒÆ?®†¥ Ø?[]{~§¶™ƒÅ©ß
µ„…–;:_Ç'*^'¡+´Ç,.- ¢#@|\ªº¬?

1. VIEWS	2. RANKING	3.RATING	4. TIEMPO	5. INFO	6. ABUSE	7. HOUYHNHNER
·}}}	᙭	★	◷	ⓘ	⌐	·}

8. STANDBY	8. HOUY	9. RECOMMEND	10.COFFE ROOM	11. VOLUMEN	12. MY ACOUNT	13. FAQ
{S*}	{h*}	☺	☕	?	h^MY	FAQ

14. CONTROL	20. FAB	15. VOTAR (RATE)	16. INVITAR AMIGO	17. VIDEO COMMENT	18. SUGGESTS	19. SEARCH
◁ ▷ ▷ II	{!}	⟂	·}{·	◎	oO	Q

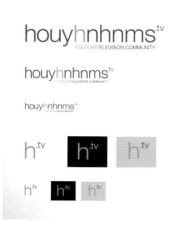

houyhnhnms.tv
YOUR ARTELEVISION COMMUNITY

i'mahouyhnhner!

i'mahouyhnhner!

i'mahouyhnhner!

inspire the world,
it can be changed.
i'mahouyhnhner!

...▸

Title: **Branding & icons design for Houyhnhnms.tv (internet broadcasting) for Arroba Networks, Spain {2007}**
Medium: **Web Design, Art direction, concept, graphic design, and illustrations**
Credits and Rationale:
This is a beautiful project, an internet broadcast with the focus on art films, short films, films festivals, for creators and audiences alike, a kind of film archive but with updatable by the users, you can vote, rank, or select films. Interesting concept by Joan Jimenez and the support and development from Arroba Networks, and Tea Time Studio (on art direction and design).All the icons and sign illustrations were created using logo type face forms. http://www. houyhnhnms.tv

IORI
HOTEL . RESTO . SHOP
いをりホテル、レストラン、ショップ

iORi HOTEL / RESTO / SHOP

iORi HOTEL . RESTO . SHOP
いをりホテル、レストラン、ショップ

iORi HOTEL / RESTO / SHOP

iORi HOTEL & BAR
ホテル＆バー

iORi HOTEL & BAR
ホテル＆バー

iORi HOTEL & BAR
ホテル＆バー

S1 TOKYO 東京スイート	HOMBRES 男	BAR バー	DUCHA シャワー
S2 OSAKA 大阪スイート	MUJERES 女	DESAYUNO 朝食	P PARKING 駐車場
R1 SAKURA 桜ルーム	GUARDA ESQUI スキールーム	COCINA キッチン	H HOTEL ホテル

Do not disturb
寝ています

iORi HOTEL & BAR
ホテル＆バー

Make up rooms
掃除
お願いします

iORi HOTEL & BAR
ホテル＆バー

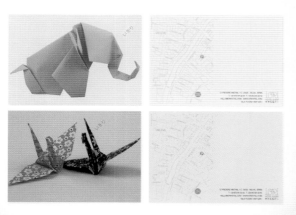

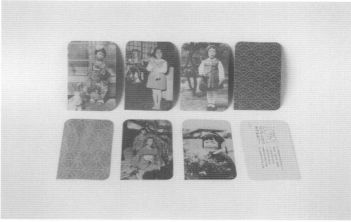

←··· ↑

Title: **Branding design for Iori Hotel, Resto & Shop {Japanese hotel & restaurant located at Vielha, Spain 2008}**
Medium: **Art direction, concept, graphic design and illustrations**
Credits and Rationale:

Iori is a Japanese style hotel, restaurant, & shop at Pirineos Catalanes, at Vielha city. For this particular project Tea Time developed the global identity, including the logo, icons, stationary, pins, packaging, signs, gadgets, website, and more... The bunny image is inspired by a Japanese traditional "Image of the rabbit in the moon" that every year is celebrated to bring prosperity to everyone. All the icons and sign illustrations were created using the logo type face forms.

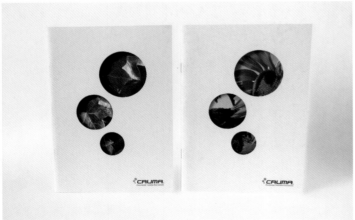

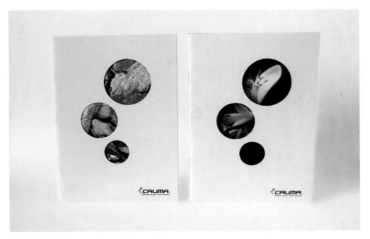

Title: **Cruma's catalogs,
calendars and CDs**
Medium: **Art direction, concept,
graphic design, and illustrations**
Dimension: **A5 and CD size**
Credits and Rationale:
**Cover design and concept for
Cruma's catalogs (a company
that produces air cleaning
machines). Editorial design and
concept for Cruma calendars
and CDs.**

KULT

CULTURA DE VIDEOJUEGOS

MAGIA EN TU SWING

EL TÍTULO DE TECMO ES UN JUEGO PARA PASAR UN BUEN RATO DE MANERA DISTENDIDA, DISFRUTÁNDOLO SÓLO O, MUCHO MEJOR, EN COMPAÑÍA.

SIRVIENDO PARA GANAR

Nuevas emociones

RETROSPECTIVA PLAYSTATION   PS1=CYAN PS2=MAG PS3=GRIS

JUEGOS TONTOS EXTREMADAMENTE ADICTIVOS

Title: **KULT MAGAZINE No. 4, 5 & 6**
Medium: **Art direction, concept, graphic design, and illustrations**
Dimension: **27.5 × 23 cm**
Credits and Rationale:
Editorial design for KULT Magazine No.4, 5 & 6

Title: **Poems "Tabla Periodica"**
Medium: **Book design**
Dimension: **A5**
Credits and Rationale:
Editorial design for the book of poems "Tabla Periodica" by Caro-lina Jobbági. Edited by BECAS ANTORCHA / TSE TSE EDITORIAL Argentina {2003}. Poetry book based on the periodic table of elements.

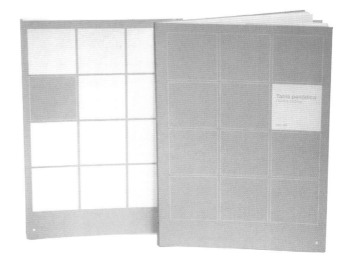

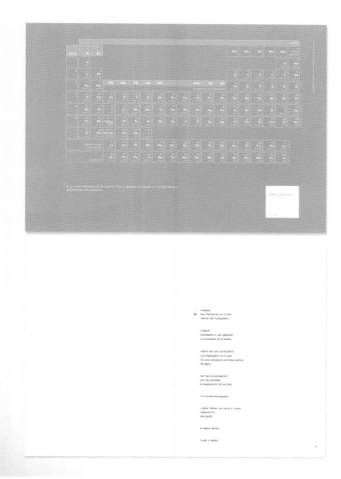

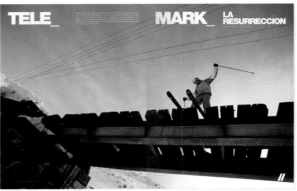

↕

Title: **The magazine of SKI REVOLUTION (01 TO 08)**

Medium: **Art direction, concept, graphic design, and illustrations**

Dimension: **30 × 23 cm**

Credits and Rationale:

Editorial design for the magazine SKI REVOLUTION (01 TO 08)

···→

Title: **The Magazine SKATEBOARDING "UNO" 18 & 22**

Medium: **Art direction, concept, graphic design, and illustrations**

Dimension: **28.5 × 23.5 cm**

Credits and Rationale:

Editorial design for the magazine SKATEBOARDING "UNO" 18 & 22. Number 18 is a tribute to the pop and Helvetica culture, Number 22 was made half & half by Sebastian Litmanovich & Sebastian Saavedra and is a tribute to the Daily Mirror style.

OPINION!

Cuando por algo no puedes salir a patinar ...impotencia.

(Más)TXT: Ruru FOTO: Sebas&tián

ALTAVOZ! JUGUETES!

Esta es una nueva sección dedicada a nuevas maneras de gastarte la pasta...

profile:

¡TU también puedes dar tu opinión!

¡A QUE ESPERAS!

¡TODOS DEBERIAN SER ABOLIDOS!

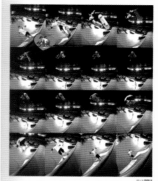

¿Un **premio** de 30.000 dólares **americanos?**

World Cup of Skateboarding
Autor de Helge Tscharn

Clasificaciones final:

"ME DA ENERGIA ESTE RITMO DE VIDA"...

"ODIO CUALQUIER TIPO DE SOPA Y CUALQUIER TIPO DE PASTEL"

helge tscharn

disfrutad...

"ASI QUE PASAN COSAS CON LAS VECINAS DE ABAJO... MUCHAS RISAS!"

CAPRICHITOS!

M:Robe 100 de Olympus
reproductor Mp3 5Gb

Mr. Xeli lo compró en Japón por unos 180 €

Jacob & Co
JC - M10

a 38.000 €
...otro caprichismo creado por JACOB.

Chrysler 300C

a 32.000 €
...lo tienes en tus MANOS...

¡EN EXCLUSIVA UNO!

"Buscaba una ciudad diferente... ...ME ENCANTA ESPAÑA" Anthony López

Entrevista y fotos: Ivan Jimenez

¡¡TIENEN MUCHAS HORMONAS PARA QUEMAR!!

INTRO!

Hola Don Pepito!

STAFF!

UNO022!

¡ES CULPA DEL ALCALDE?

UNO HOT LINE
+34 253 17 74

UNO! ANTES QUE NADIE • UNO! ANTES QUE NADIE • UNO! ANTES QUE NADIE • UNO! ANTES QUE NADIE

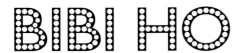

Can you please briefly tell us when and how you started "crossover" design? Also how "crossover" design impacted your design style and beliefs at work?

Being a company that focuses on results-driven ideas, we were looking for a fresh approach to take on an old brand. Some questions included how we might increase the brands value and perception that had shaped the brand over the years. Hence, we started with an idea to bring old brands in to the new. It is not so much about a design style but an approach. We were looking at something that is true to the hearts of many in China based on familiarity and an emotional connection. The approach dictated the crossover. We have a strong belief that an old brand has in itself a respectable history that can have a significant impact on the present. That belief drove us to think outside the box. We took the initiative to become pro-active and to put our ideas to work.

What is your view of the current trend of "crossover" design? For example, will the emergence of "crossover" design make the current separation of work boundaries fuzzy? Why? Will "crossover" affect the professionalism of design work?

Crossover presents an interesting way to merge the best of each practice into a new form. There are many forms including those of East/West, New/Old etc. What separates crossover from the pack is the ability to think beyond the ordinary. It's like mutation but with a visual art-form that has a new language which is understood by the audience. Crossover isn't a blurred vision nor is it a gray line of existence. With crossover, it demands an even more detailed presentation of every element. It has to be distinctive in its expression based on a new design language. This language is one that crosses over traditional boundaries. Simply put, the visual foundation has to be firm before an attempt is to be made.

What is your work plan in the future?

The future is bright. We are already planning our next creative collaboration by looking at active interaction through alternate gaming reality. By creating experiences that are "real," we hope to bring about a change in perception. At the end of the day, it has to combine elements of fun and new discoveries for all of us.

Name: Bibi Ho
Company: AMg Digital Lab
Country: China
Email: bibi.ho@amusegroup.com
Website: www.amusegroup.com
www.amusegroup.com/labs

Bio:
Bibi Ho is a product designer by training. His career spans over a decade covering multiple disciplines linking the art of creative expression. Bibi started as a graphic designer and later moved to EURO RSCG as an Art Director. In his advertising career, he has worked on many world-class brands such as Philips, Dell, Singapore Telecom, Alcatel, Volvo, & Djarum. This foundation and understanding of brands has seen him pioneering EURO RSCG's Interactive Design department. At the turn of the Millennium, his entrepreneurial spirit caught up with him. At the height of the dotcom period, together with two other partners, they started The Ad Inc- a firm that focuses on through-the-line communications from TVC, integrated marketing to interactive. Later that year, The Ad Inc was acquired by the World's leading digital marketing group, AKQA. By the end of 2001, he had moved to Paris where he took up a pastry course at the renowned culinary academy, Le Cordon Bleu. There, he explored another way to fulfill his appetite for another form of creative expression. In 2004, he was offered the opportunity to set up the Beijing branch of XM – a leading Interactive Communication company in Asia. His role as Managing Director/Creative Director had begun.

Title: **Re:born**

...›

Title: **Re:born**

Credits and Rationale:

Project Re:born is a creative initiative to bring old Chinese brands into the new. It is an attempt to re-establish the presence of old Chinese brands by opening up new doors of discovery to a generation of young Chinese consumers.

It is neither a rebranding exercise nor is it a total reconstruction. But rather, it is one that takes a look into the cultural context based on the brand history and its development that has captured the hearts of many Chinese consumers through the times.

The Essence of Project Re:born are Truth, Honesty, Respect, Imagination, Innovation, Freshness, Creativity, Originality, Flair, Chinese-ness. Time has changed but the spirit remains. Project Re:born hopes to breed new life to old Chinese brands. A new image. A new perspective. A new discovery. It relates to facts taken from history both culturally and economically. It reveals a path that has a significant influence to an era of people who had previously came in contact with the brand. Project Re:born is looking to break through the clutter and allowing this nouveau generation to take a step back and appreciate the past. In doing so, the past will provide a foundation for discovering newer existence for them. Thus, it forms a uniquely "Chinese-ness" in a world where the old and new co-exist.

Web: http://reborn.amusegroup.com

←··· ↕
Title: **Re:born**

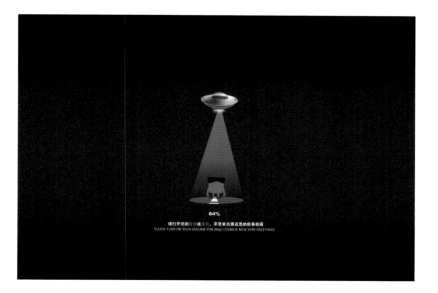

Title: **Piggy Pop Talk**
Medium: **Graphic, Web, Clay Models, Photography**
Credits and Rationale:

Originally conceived for Lunar New Year back in 2007, we have experimented using handmade clay characters and voice recording to produce an eCard that combined design & technology. It was the year of the Pig. The Chinese name (Zhu-Bao-Hang) suggests with a pun of a jewelry shop. The creative execution used a vending machine concept to link all the design elements together. The eCard allows users to DIY their own creations from choosing the different clay characters to customizing your own background icons to adding your own recorded voices and inputting your own text. The final step is simply blasting if off to those who needed a dose of piggy's magic. A total of 10 clay hand-made piglets characters were created, with each their own distinctive style and unique looks. The rest was left to the user's imagination and creativity. Users were able to create a simple greeting based on the "conversations" of two clay characters. The end result is a personalized eCard that has your choice of clay characters that speaks to your recipient with your own voice. We had also organized a contest to reward the most creative eCard based on their viewership. The winner gets an iPod for their efforts.
Now, who says an eCard doesn't talk back?

Title: **HP tx2000 Laptop PC**

Medium: **Viral Video, Web, Photography, Dance Recruitment Event, Contest**

Dimension: **N.A.**

Credits and Rationale:

HP tx2000: Twist, Write and Touch – Giving you all the moves you desire
The brief was simple: Create a contest that engages the users through
their own generated content. Users join in the dance contest, then watch
and vote their winners.

Unlike most traditional Web-enabled contest, this one takes in the form
of getting users to take part in a real dance contest. Dancers have to
perform based on the 3 key features of the new HP tx2000 Laptop –
Twist, Write or Touch. Video recording of their dances were posted online,
allowing audiences to watch and vote. Amidst the clutter of getting one to
create their original content, we opted to video their dance performance
and put in on the Web on their behalf. The results is a contest website
that is dedicated to an unbias attributes of a true-to-life expression.

The combination of digital and event-led elements had made it possible
to generate a buzz among the audiences. The contest site also allowed
audiences to leave their comments.

Through such form of entertainment, we were able to draw crowds
of followers for this contest. Plus, it has proved that assisting content
generation by participant lowered the barrier to entry.

Title: **Neu Brand Kid**
Medium: **Product, Graphic, Web, Photography**
Credits and Rationale:

Neu Brand Kid project was an initiative to discover the connection between brands and a single element. Originally derived from a promotional campaign with one of our clients whereby a series of 4 toys were created for the promotion; based on a standard form, each with a theme of its own–Play, Work, Fun, Cool.

The project led to an internal exploration of how personality and character may be represented through a distinctive element. Hence, the birth of the "Brand Kid."

This project brief challenged the creative team to interpret the character of each brand may be represented by the "Brand Kid." Each team member was given a brand to work with. Based on their understanding, they got down to the drawing board and give these "Brand Kids" a life of their own.

The result is an interesting mix of how Chinese designers interpret brands of the world. Their perception and knowledge of these brands create a unique blend of visual representations.

DHNN

Can you please briefly tell us when and how you started "crossover" design? Also how "crossover" design impacted your design style and beliefs at work?

We think that art is the mother of design, crossover design is a side effect of design, it impacts on us like a momentary exit, to relax, and design freely without many rules and deadlines.

What is your view of the current trend of "crossover" design? For example, will the emergence of "crossover" design makes the current separation of work boundary fuzzy? Why? Will "cross over" affect the professionalism of design work?

Crossover design doesn't exist at all for us. Design is functionality; we take "crossover" design as an expression, for us and for the workflow—nothing more.

What is your work plan in the future?

Be happy.

Name: Lucas Davison, Juan Crescimone
Company: DHNN (Design has no name)
Country: Argentina
Email: info@dhnn.com.ar
Web: www.dhnn.com.ar

Bios:
DHNN is an independent visual comunications Studio, established in Buenos Aires, Argentina, in 2007. Our main aim is to provide each project with the best of our creative potential, and we are built around a shared belief that great design can make good ideas into extraordinary ones. We are a multidisciplinary studio that develops efficient communication systems based on strategic, efficient investigation and research.

◄···
Title: **Motorcycle**
Medium: **Printed**
Credits and Rationale:
We love motorcycles, and this is a radiography of one of them.

···►
Title: **TyperArt**
Medium: **Printed**
Credits and Rationale:
We love Carson.

Para crecer con todo. Modo de preparación

225cm3+32,5g = 250cm3.

Calcio. Proteínas. Vitaminas A y D.

Manejar el contenido

Mantener el envase cerrado en lugar fresco

Rinde 3 litros. Peso neto 400g.

con utensilios perfectamente

LOTE 323 4359

y seco. No exponer a la luz solar.

limpios.

Colocá una cucharadita colmada

(**1.5g**)

de café por taza (750ml)

INCORPORÁ AGUA POTABLE A

punto de hervir. agrega azúcar

Confianza.

Fueron 75 años compartiendo *a gusto.*

vitamina

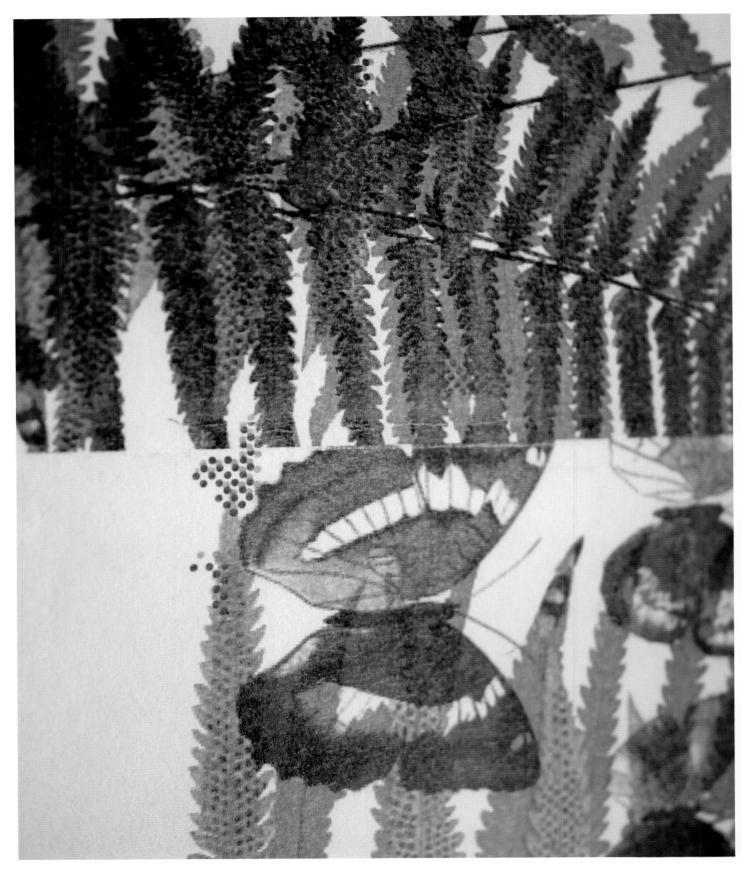

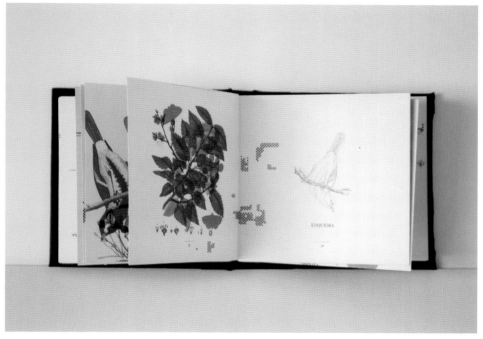

←··· ↑
Title: **Botanical Morphologic Exploration**
Medium: **Printed**
Credits and Rationale:
40 pages book, analysis about butterflies, birds, plants, and colours.

Title: **Beck 8-bit Variations**
Medium: **Offset Printed Package**
Credits and Rationale:

We love music, and we love videogames, we think that this is one of the best combinations in our life. With this project, we attempted to develop a special edition (in fact, a prototype edition) for a nonexistent Beck record. The concept: 8-Bit videogames. We came across this concept by listening to a series of Beck's remixes, where the sounds took us back to those abandon ware games, very common during the 80s. With this in mind, we imagined a particular aesthetic that could, later on, become a special edition of the artist's remixes. As a result, the materialization of the concept presented an 80s aesthetic, with a lot of colour, highly contrasting fuchsia colours and pixel-art-like characters. The materialization includes, as well, a NES cartridge, which contains the record. Through this prototype, we attempted to recreate the possibility that's hardly ever seen nowadays in the disco graphic industry: more integrated package when buying music. In other words, it's not just about the music, but the whole universe that comes along with it.

↕ ↕
Title: **Collage to save the world**
Medium: **Recycle Paper stuff**
Credits and Rationale:
**We think that trash created
by the people could be art, we
use it, and make inspirational
artworks.**

↕
Title: **Wall properties intervention**
Medium: **Installation**
Credits and Rationale:
**Installation about the real estate
business, with papers, danger
tapes, plot designs, etc.**

Title: **Textual complexity**

Medium: **Plotted**

Credits and Rationale:

This piece is a combination of 1 million and 368 characters in perfect harmony.

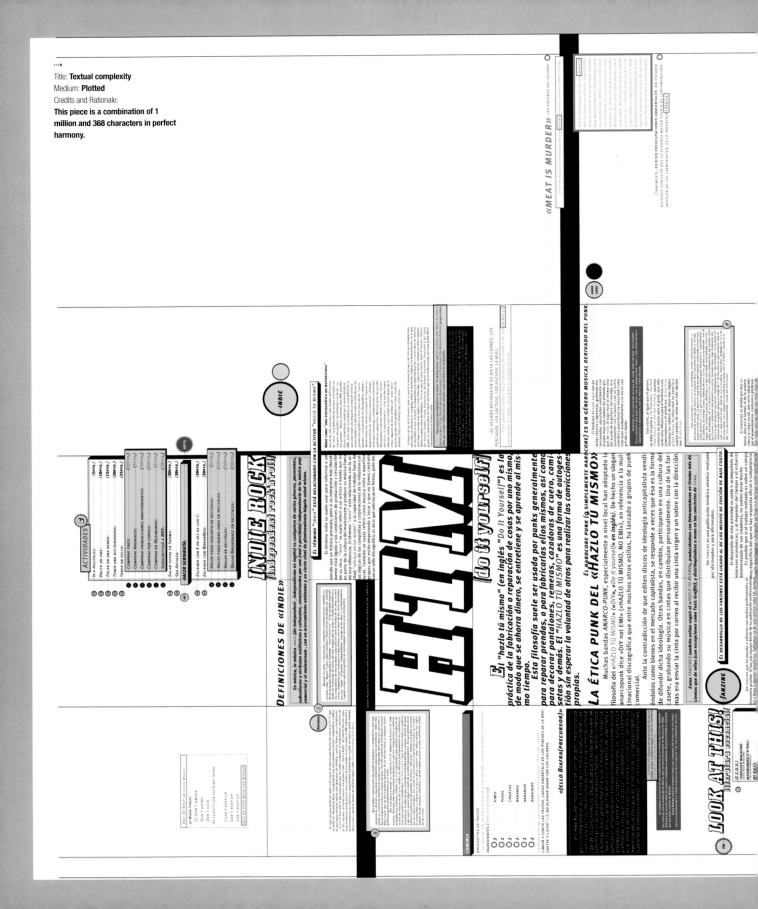

CLUB DEL PUNK

A finales de los setenta, la escena HARDCORE en Washington DC atraía a bastante gente. Bastantes hardcores cayeron en la heroína y a las salas de conciertos sólo podían entrar personas mayores de 21 años para proteger a los menores de los daños del abuso de alcohol. La única excepción eran los llamados conciertos ALL AGES ('TODAS LAS EDADES').

En esos conciertos, se ponía una "X" a los menores en el dorso de las manos, pintadas con un rotulador negro indeleble, para evitar que consiguieran alcohol. Con esa "X" se les podía identificar fácilmente como menores de edad en la barra.

Por lo cual, tomaron la iniciativa y fundaron sus propios grupos. Empezaron a reivindicar el uso de las "X" contra el uso de drogas. Empezaron a difundir otras ideas que consideraban mucho más constructivas que el mensaje típico de las bandas de punk el aquel momento. Fue entonces cuando surgió el HARDCORE STRAIGHT EDGE (HC SXE).

Se estilo se caracterizó por canciones con mensajes directos contra las drogas.

VEGANISMO [vegetarian]

Un vegano es alguien que no consume productos o subproductos de origen animal, o productos testados sobre animales.
El término original inglés 'VEGAN' fue ideado en Londres en 1944 por 7 vegetarianos que se unieron para crear la Vegan Society, que sigue activa en Inglaterra. Utilizaron la 3 primeras letras y las dos últimas de la palabra VEGETARIAN para formar la palabra VEGAN.

PUNTAJES

0-100	DEFINITIVAMENTE NO ES LO TUYO.
100-200	LARGO CAMINO DEBES DE RECORRER.
200-300	EMPIEZA A ENTENDER.
300-400	ENTRAS.
400-500	ENTRAS Y LO VIVES.
500-600	HARDCORE
600-700	CALI HARDCORE
700-800	PUNK
800-900	PUNK FAMOSO
900-1000	SUPERCRAK

APARIENCIAS

TENER TATUAJES:	(5 PTS.)
TENER TATUAJE DE LA OVEJITA DE MINOR:	(15 PTS.)
TENER TATUAJE DE THE CRASS:	(20 PTS.)
TENER PIERCINGS:	(5 PTS.)

MODO DE SER

STRAIGHT EDGE:	(20 PTS.)
STRAIGHT EDGE (POR MÁS DE 5 AÑOS):	(50 PTS.)
EX STRAIGHT EDGE:	(5 PTS.)
NUNCA STRAIGHT EDGE:	(10 PTS.)
PUNK (POR MÁS DE 5 AÑOS):	(50 PTS.)

ACTIVIDADES (EXTRACURRICULARES)

IR AL PARQUE RIVADAVIA LOS DOMINGOS:	(15 PTS.)
IR A LA FERIA DE FANZINES EN CONGRESO:	(15 PTS.)
ANDAR EN SKATE CON TABLA DE LOS OCHENTAS:	(20 PTS.)
ANDAR EN ROLLER:	(20 PTS.)
ANDAR EN BICICLETA:	(20 PTS.)
ANDAR A PIE:	(5 PTS.)
TENER BANDERA DE VINILOS:	(5 PTS.)
JUGAR AL ATARI:	(20 PTS.)

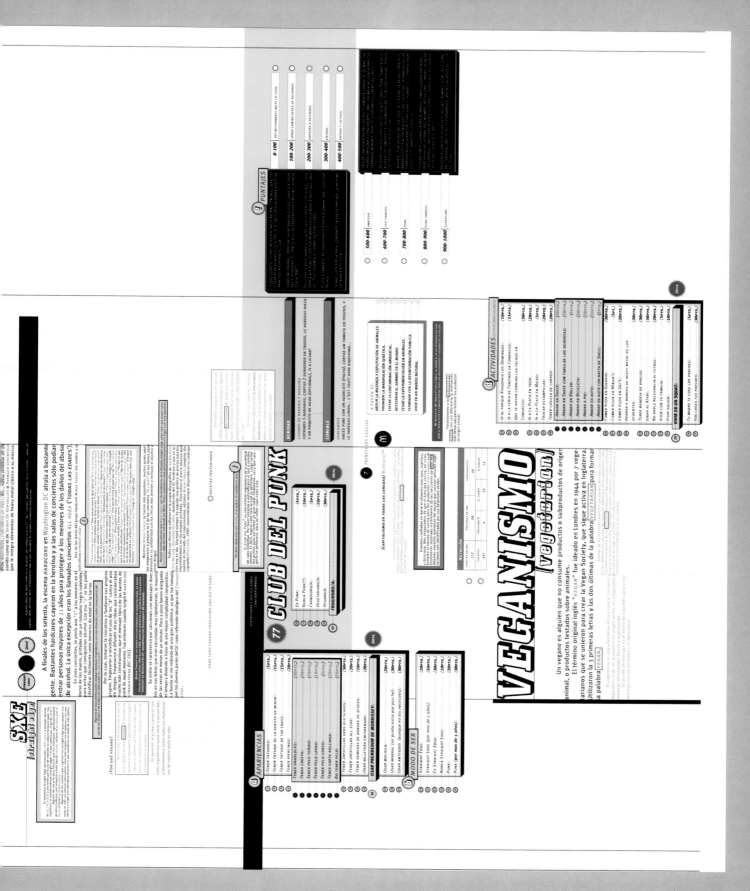

Title: **Geekmilk Project**
Medium: **Printed**
Credits and Rationale:

**The idea for this project was
born from the proposal of an
online publication, whose
theme was the concept of
geek, nerd, and so on. We
decided to produce and direct
a photographic shoot. In a few
words, our idea was to link the
nerdish world to the fantasies
that are generally associated to
that kind of person. Therefore,
we used a female model and
bathed her in milk.**

Title: **Neighborhood**
Medium: **Printed**
Credits and Rationale:
**Collage work trying to tell the life of a
peaceful neighborhood.**

Title: **70s Gamming Retro**
Medium: **Digital**
Credits and Rationale:
**Vintage memories of abandoned
arcade videogames.**

Title: **Randomize**
Medium: **Printed**
Credits and Rationale:
**Random experimentation with
shapes and colour.**

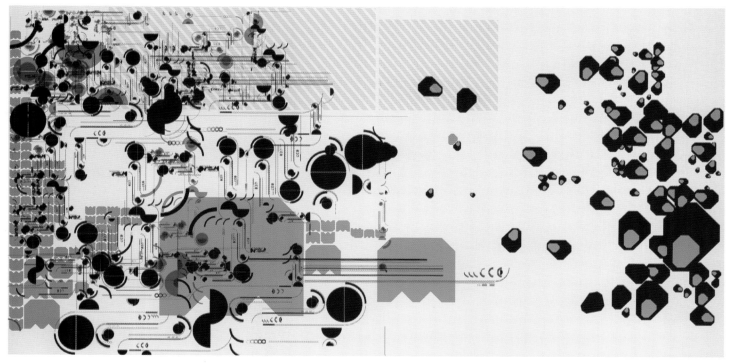

Title: **Geekmilk Project**

Medium: **Printed**

Credits and Rationale:

The idea for this project was born from the proposal of an online publication, which theme was the concept of geek, nerd, and so on. We decided to produce and direct a photographic shoot. In few words, our idea was to link the nerdish world to the fantasies that are generally associated to that kind of person. Therefore, we called a female model and bathed her in milk.

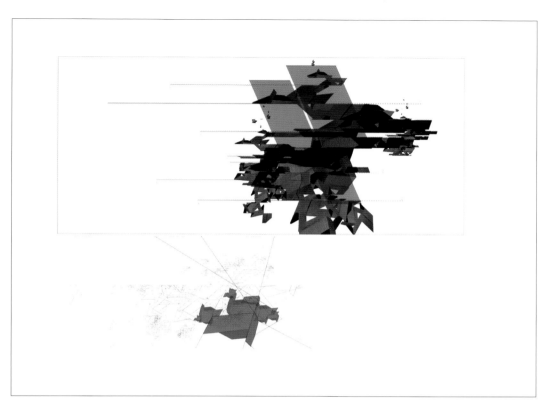

↕ ←⋯

Title: **Scheme Sightseen Series**
Medium: **Printed**
Credits and Rationale:

What we attempted to do through this project was to create a hypothesis of movement, in the context of a process of morphological research. We studied and developed a morphological scheme and then put it into action, trying to imagine its own logic and relationship to the shapes. The first rough outline of the scheme emerges from a scale model in balsa wood, studying the shapes of crystals and different references where the forms are generated or facetted shapes come from (crystals, quartz, etc). We prepared a large number of scale models until we got to the level of depuration of the one on display. Afterwards, we tried to digitally generate different manifestations of movement, an animation acting out the different manifestations of these shapes. Once we were through with testing and developing the animation of movement, we developed a series of different montages, integrating the existing shapes and the ones we've artificially generated to the real world. We did this by inserting the images in to photos of the city, trying to transmit in as realistic a way as possible how these shapes would be if they really existed: what size would they be, how would they move around.

STUDIOHOBO

Can you please briefly tell us when and how you started "crossover" design? Also how "crossover" design impacted your design style and beliefs at work?

We both came from different fields not related to design. Cintya is a plastics artist and I am a contemporary percussionist, maybe we have a lot of crossover feeling in our blood. When we started to work with graphic design and crafts we brought them all together, therefore I think our work was born with the "crossover" concept. We believe that thinking in a broader way, accepting different languages will prevent us from falling into empty speech.

What is your view of the current trend of "crossover" design ? For example, will the emergence of "crossover" design make the current separation of work boundaries fuzzy? Why? Will "crossover" affect the professionalism of design work?

We think it already does. In order to make design we need to know a bunch of rules and then break them all. The way we are going to break them is through our experiences. We can't think just in "Design" to do Design. We face crossover thinking as inherent fuel for creativity, and creativity is what Design is all about.

What is your work plan in the future?

All decisions we make now will set our path to the future. Conquering spaces through a crossover-minded approach and centered in the multiplicity of being. One step at a time.

Name: Cintya Hobo & Flavio Hobo
Company: StudioHobo
Country: Portugal
Email: hello@fourillusion.com
Website: www.studiohobo.com
www.iwantmyhobo.com

Bios:
Cintya Hobo is an artist and jewelry designer. From 2000 to 2005 she was an integral part of the Arts and Brazilian Culture's research team at Itaú Cultural helping the institute in its work of mapping the high heterogeneous visual culture manifestations in Brazil. Since October 2007 Cintya Hobo has lived in Lisbon, Portugal, to take a Master in Design and Visual Culture at IADE. Flavio Hobo was born in Conselheiro Lafaiete, Minas Gerais - Brazil in 1979.His career as a designer took off in 2001, after winning a web design contest at his college while taking his bachelors degree in contemporary percussion studies.Flavio then worked as designer, musician, and studied fine arts in São Paulo, applying his knowledge of the visual and musical fields in his own works until 2003. In 2008 Cintya and Flavio created the StudioHobo (www.studiohobo.com).

···›
Title: **Zouka**
Medium: **Print**
Credits and Rationale:
Self-promotional illustration for a calendar printed in Brazil.

造花

Durum
percussão brasil

DIMENSÕES

CARLOS STASI
Dimensões
10'46"

MARIO FICARELLI
Ensaio 95
13'46"

FRANCISCO ABREU
Cá Entre Nós
8'05"

EDUARDO GUIMARÃES ÁLVARES
Pratilheiros Catapimbásticos
(Homenagem a Spike Jones
e The Slickers)
18'36"

FERNANDO CHAUB
ELO'S
11'06"

CARLOS STASI
33 Samba Zabobry
12'49"

EDUARDO GUIMARÃES ÁLVARES (1959)

Graduado em Composição pela Universidade de São Paulo, estudou com Willy Corrêa de Oliveira e Gilberto Mendes, além de Dante Greta. Em 1985 foi selecionado para a IV Bienal de Música Brasileira Contemporânea. Recebeu em 1991 o prêmio de Melhor Trilha Sonora Original para o álbum de Família de Nelson Rodrigues, com o Grupo Cellajo de Belo Horizonte. Em 1991 recebeu o primeiro Prêmio Gold Amadeus em conceito com a Bolsa Wien na Alemanha. Em 2003 foi contemplado com o primeiro prêmio na Alemanha. Em 2003 foi contemplado "O Enigma de Caim". Desde 2005, é professor da Universidade Livre de Música, no Centro de Estudos Musicais Tom Jobim em São Paulo.

PRATILHEIROS CATAPIMBÁSTICOS (HOMENAGEM A SPIKE JONES E THE SLICKERS) (1994)

(Executantes: Fernando, Leopoldo, Ricardo, Richard e Rodolfo)

Pratilheiro é o nome geralmente empregado nas bandas de música do interior para o encarregado pelos pratos de choque e Catapimbástico é um neologismo de catapimba + bombástico. Várias ideias foram estimulantes para a criação da peça: um documentário sobre Spike Jones; experiências com grupos de música cênica; espetáculos sobre textos dadaístas e admiração pela música de Edgard Varèse.

EDUARDO GUIMARÃES ÁLVARES (1959)

With a degree in Musical Composition at University of São Paulo, he studied with Willy Corrêa de Oliveira and Gilberto Mendes, as well as Dante Greta. In 1985 he was chosen for the IV Brazilian Contemporary Musical Festival. In 1991 he was awarded the Best Original Score Prize for Nelson Rodrigues's "Family Album", along with Cellajo Ensemble from Belo Horizonte. Also in 1991 he picked up the Gold Amadeus Prize in the Musik Kreativ competition, in Germany. In 2003 Álvares was awarded the Bolsa Wien de Artes for the opera "Cain's Enigma". Since 2005 he has been a professor at Free Music University, at the Tom Jobim Centre for Musical Studies in São Paulo.

PRATILHEIROS CATAPIMBÁSTICOS (HOMAGE TO SPIKE JONES AND THE SLICKERS) (1994)

(Performers: Fernando, Leopoldo, Ricardo, Richard and Rodolfo)

"Pratilheiro" is the name usually used in musical groups from countryside for the person in charge of the cymbals and "Catapimbástico" is a neologism of "catapimba" + bombastic. Several ideas acted as stimulants for the creation of the piece: a documentary on Spike Jones, experiences with groups of scenic music, shows about Dadaist texts and admiration for Edgard Varèse's music.

Title: **Durum**
Medium: **Print**
Credits and Rationale:
CD cover and booklet project for Durum Ensemble, Brazil.

Title: **Beauties I**
Medium: **Drawing**
Dimensions: **36 × 26 cm**

Title: **Beauties II**
Medium: **Pen and paper collage**
Dimensions: **30 × 19 cm**
Credits and Rationale:
The "Beauties" series is about happiness and freedom, a blend of emotions crossing through time to reveal itself.

<...

Title: **Sushi**
Medium: **Felt, synthetic leather, beads**
Dimensions: **98 × 3 × 2 cm**

·↘

Title: **Mafalda**
Medium: **Package for foodstuffs (ECAL), beads, plastic bottle caps**
Dimensions: **74 × 3 × 3 cm**

⋮

Title: **Margarida**
Medium: **Package for foodstuffs (ECAL), beads, plastic bottle caps**
Dimensions: **64 × 4 × 2 cm**

Title: **Symphony No. 1**
Medium: **Beads, cotton, wool, line, plastic carboy water**
Dimensions: **65 × 7 × 3 cm**

Title: **Symphony No. 2**
Medium: **Beads, plastic carboy water**
Dimensions: **81 × 4 × 4 cm**

Title: **Symphony No. 3**
Medium: **Plastic bag, line**
Dimensions: **53 × 7 × 3 cm**

Title: **Symphony No. 4**
Medium: **Beads, fabric, package of garlic and potatoes**
Dimensions: **65 × 2 × 2 cm**

····▸

Title: **Landscape 01**
Medium: **Acrylic on canvas**
Dimensions: **24 × 30 cm**

⋮

Title: **Landscape 02**
Medium: **Acrylic on canvas**
Dimensions: **24 × 30 cm**

...→
Title: **Hobo**
Medium: **Print**
Credits and Rationale:
Logo designed for our online store "I want my Hobo." The symbol shows the union between the syllables HO + BO written in Japanese katakana.

...→
Title: **Mixona**
Medium: **Print**
Credits and Rationale:
Logo redesign proposal for a fashion business brand based in USA.

...→
...→
Title: **Amazon**
Medium: **Print**
Credits and Rationale:
Logo redesign proposal for Amazon PC, Brazilian computer-related company.

...→
...→
Title: **Femme Comunicacao**
Medium: **Print**
Credits and Rationale:
Logo designed for a brand new agency focused on marketing to women.

◄···
Title: **Zampronha & Moralez**
Medium: **Print**
Credits and Rationale:
Poster for an electroacoustic and contemporary percussion music concert

Title: **Afroditte**
Medium: **Print**
Credits and Rationale:
Bag for Afroditte's shoes store

PARSIL STUDIO™

Can you please briefly tell us when and how you started "crossover" design? Also how "cross over" design impacted your design style and believes at work?

When I was at university I had some contacts to the movie industry and airplane design, I am really interested in music, I have attempted many kinds of media manifestation. I graduated at the beginning of the ''crossover'' period. I start with many design cooperation that was involved with many areas of design, it was at that time that I founded 96k™, then I started to contact world famous customers. The creative process also becomes more active. Cross media design has greatly increased my experience which is getting richer everyday. It has helped me to develop a much wider customer base. In 2008 me and my friends decided to build a bigger Parsil studio™.

What is your view of the current trend of "crossover" design? For example, will the emergence of "crossover" design makes the current separation of work boundary fuzzy? Why? Will "cross over" affect the professionalism of design work?

I do not like hard and fast design, design must diversify to diversify the structure of knowledge, and to create such designs would be different. "Crossover" design depends on the designer's own qualities and training, this would enable them to better respond to a variety of issues. Relative to professional design I prefer "crossover" design.

What is your work plan in the future?

That better designers and studios conduct broader cross-media cooperation. This world belongs to "crossover " design.

Name: Liuzheng (96k)
Company: 96k™ | Creative boutique & Parsil studio™
Country: China
Email: about96@hotmail.com
Web: www.96k.com.cn

Bio:

96k's name: Liu Zheng. 96k was born in a port city of developing country (CHINA), deeply influenced in his childhood by different foreign cultures and religions, he threw himself both into the exotic & traditional arts, At an early age, adoring sprinting, he was trained to be a professional sprinter; however, for many reasons he had to quit, and in the future, he focused all his energy on art. As most artists who pursue liberty, he stopped his school life to start his own art career after graduating from university. In 2005, 96k came to Beijing, created 96k™ Creative Boutique, involving graphic design, motion graphics, print design, website design, 96k has worked for these clients: Nike/ Idn/ Tiger/ SonyEricsson/ PEPSI/ Motorola/ Microsoft/ INTER/ Lenovo/ eBay/ adFunture/ WangFeng/ Coldtea/ ZhengJun/ CCTV/ CETV/ Dazhongyule/ Shandong TV/ ChinaMob/ ARRTCO/ Buffalo/ Perfect Life/ Casa&design/ Abitare/ HP/ LG and Cadburys. He was also creating & managing an entertainment company. In 2008, Liuzheng got together with 96k™ & Layer™ & Usion™3 Multimedia Studios along with designer Bing Xu they founded a Parsil studio™, where they are engaged in Graphic Design, Motion Graphics, Web Design, Branding & Typography, Print Design, Music Production, Sound Design, Film. Parsil studio™. There are 5 different media players and core designers. Some of the people are the core of the predecessor of the 4A Company such as the senior art director. They have a wealth of experience. They have a special talent and are in every field to ensure that their works are fashionable and up to date.

Title: **Branding & Typography**

Medium: **Adobe Illustrator**

Credits and Rationale:

Parsil studio™ designs logos for many Chinese design studio and brands. Its design style is avant-garde and fashionable. Antares is a technology company in China; emerging enterprises believe that technology is strength. "Old yin sheep soup" has a long history in China, Parsil studio™ Designed the logo for a very successful store, it blends modern and ancient Chinese elements, it has brought new life and recognition to the store.

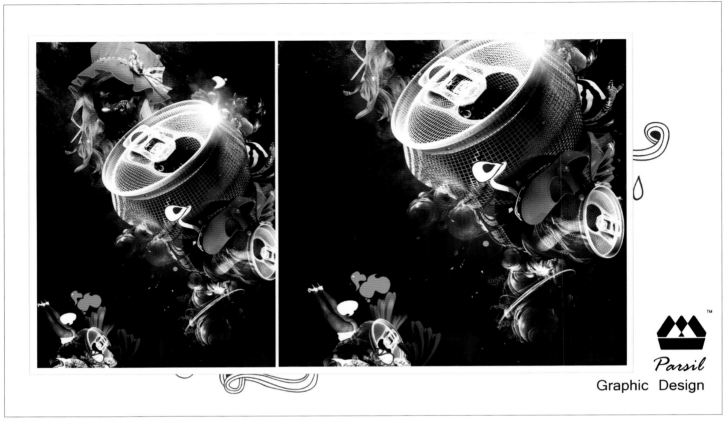

‹···
···›

Title: **Graphic Design Cocacola**
Medium: **Collage, Graphic Design, Three dimensional modeling, Typeface design, Plane design, Illustration, Special effect synthesis**
Credits and Rationale:

Cocacola is an international brand; this storyboard shows a conceptual illustration. This form is different from the former traditional illustrations, this time we used three dimensional software simulation to create the scene first. Then we put the three dimensional graphics into re-modeling software, the addition of the film's special effects synthesis, appears to be more surreal.

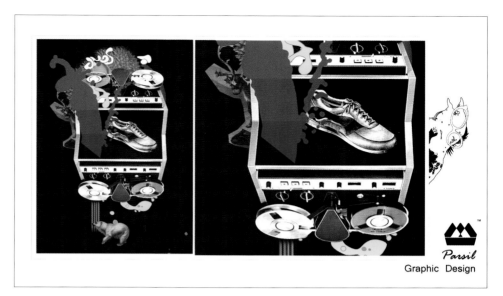

Graphic Design

Graphic Design

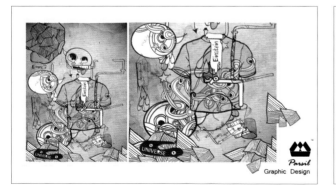

Graphic Design

Graphic Design

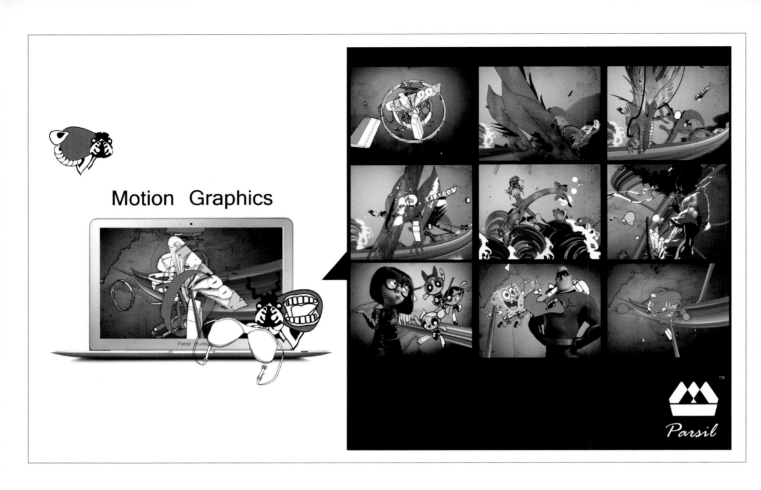

Motion Graphics

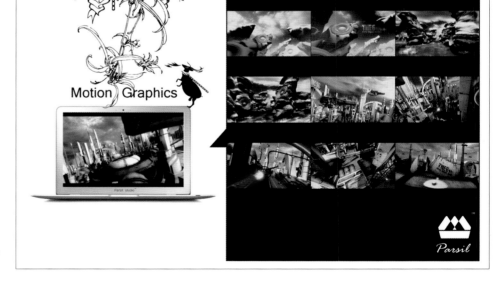

Motion Graphics

Title: **Motion Graphics_ARRTCO**

Medium: **Mix illustration, Graphic Design, Three-dimensional animation, Sound Design, Typeface design, Special effect synthesis**

Credits and Rationale:

This large project uses the mix of illustration and design as a Paste picture, the entire event occurs in a hypothesized three-dimensional space. The camera unceasingly shuttles back and forth from space which seeks ARRTCO's logo. Finally the waterdrop animation reveals the ARRTCO logo.

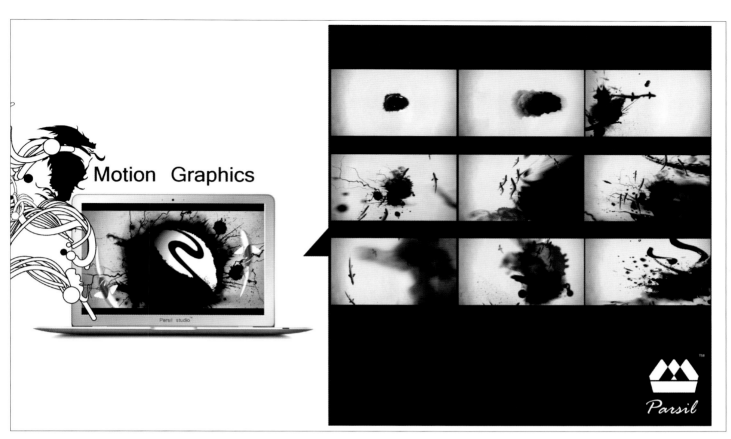

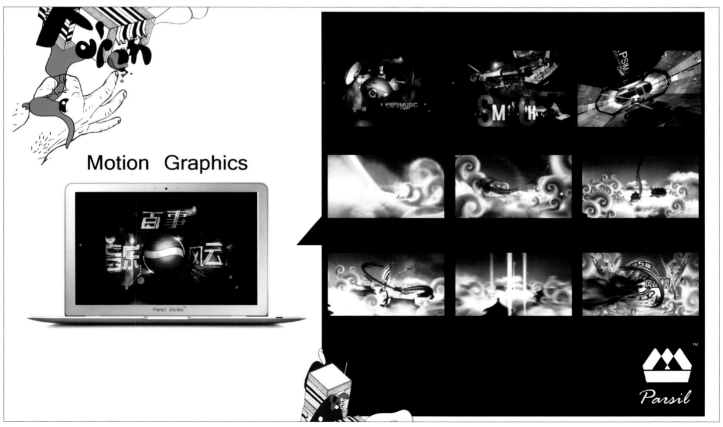

215

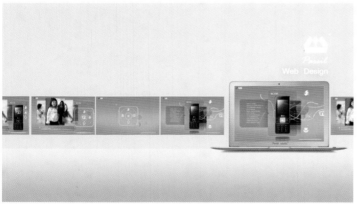

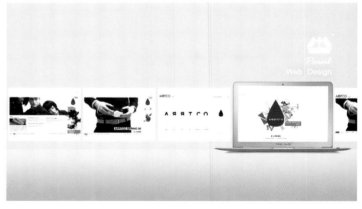

Title: **Web Design**

Medium: **Adobe Photoshop, Adobe Illustrator, Autodesk 3ds Max, Adobe After Effects, Adobe Flash**

Credits and Rationale:

Parsil studio™ web design customers include: LG, EMI, HP, Publicis Group and other international clients, including the biggest Chinese movie investment Limited company Huayi Brothers, fashion brands such as Arrtco etc. Mr Hu Yanbin who is one of the most popular entertainers in EMI China, EMI finds Parsil studio™ to design official website to promote Hu Yanbin.The website combines many forms: video, illustration, Interactive games etc, it fully expresses Parsil studios™ rich abilities in cross-border design.

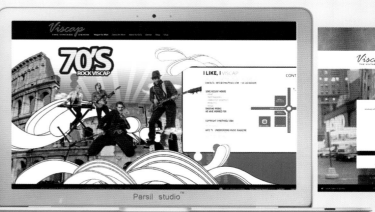

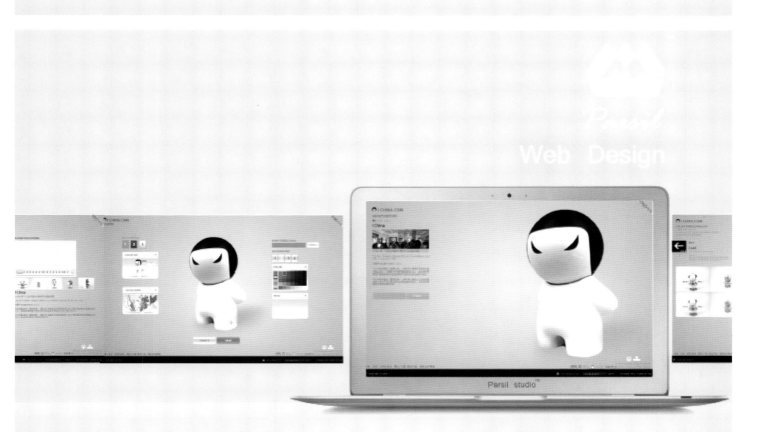

RENI WONG

Can you please briefly tell us when and how you started "crossover" design? Also how "crossover" design impacted your design style and beliefs at work?

I started to do crossover design because some brands found some of my character designs suitable for their own branding. It didn't impact me on my style and beliefs much, because I have always been this way, which is doing what I want to do.

What is your view of the current trend of "crossover" design? For example, will the emergence of "crossover" design make the current separation of work boundaries fuzzy? Why? Will "crossover" affect the professionalism of design work?

Nowadays you can see so much "crossover" all around the world and many of them are already boring. Crossover won't affect the professionalism of design work, but the tastes of clients do. It happens all the time.

What is your work plan in the future?

I will concentrate more on comics and graphic novels. If possible I want to try some character designs for games.

Name: Reni Wong
Company: Jump And Hop Studio
Country: Hong Kong, China
Email: direnio@gmail.com
Web: www.jumpnhop.com

Bio:
Born; 1987 – Age: 21 years old, together with two other friends formed "Jump & Hop." From then on, being in the creative field became his career. 1993 - Was bold to turn down a place at University; after graduating, he practiced his drawing skills like a maniac. 1998- Due to his passion for illustration, he became a freelance illustrator and an art teacher for children. 2003- Referred by a friend to work as an art director for Dribbling Toys International. Started to design for stationary and toys, most of it was bean bag toys. 2005- Became the art director and illustrator for Xin publishing company, He was also the art director for Fallen Angels.
2007- Jump & Hop became official, and worked together with Xin Publishing and Fallen Angels on a contract basis. Working in comics, toys, and also writing for various magazines. In the same year, was invited by Taiwanese toy master Tony Lin to become an administrative assistant. - Crossover with Asian pop star Jay Chow. Designed two T-shirts of the famous character "Smartan," which crossed over with Jay Chow's shop "Omni."

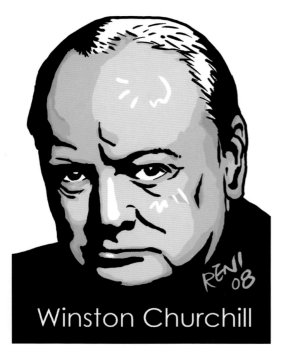

Winston Churchill

⟨··· ···⟩
Title: **Portrait Series**
Medium: **Graphics**
Credits and Rationale:
Personal works,
These are the drawings that I
use for practice.

Al Pacino

RENI 08

Title: **Portrait Series**
Medium: **Graphics**
Credits and Rationale:
Personal works,
Personal works, These are the
drawings that I use for practice.

Title: **Portrait Series**
Medium: **Graphics**
Credits and Rationale:
Personal works,
These are the drawings that I use for practice.

VENOM. THE CROW.

Be my slave!

RENI 08

RENI 08

RENI 08

RENI

P1

P2

P3

P4

←···
Title: **Reiki p1 – p4**
Medium: **Comics**
Credits and Rationale:
**Comics for Reiki the Movie,
directed by Pedro Chaves.**

⋮
Title: **Phase#1 - #2**
Medium: **Comics**
Credits and rationale:
**Two page comic for Taiwan
magazine "X-CUP".**

Title: **Smartan vol 13a – 13b**
Medium: **Comics**
Credits and Rationale:
**Smartan comics for East Touch
magazine, Hong Kong.**

…▸
Title: **Reiki the Movie**
Medium: **Postcard (graphic)**
Credits and Rationale:
**Postcard design for a Belgium
movie "Reiki" directed by Pedro
Chaves.**

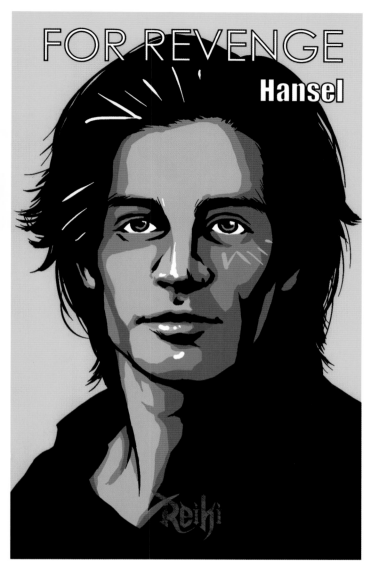

FOR REVENGE
Hansel

FOR KNOWLEDGE
Glass

FOR JUSTICE
Ant

FOR LOVE
Vann

FOR FREEDOM
Reisha

FOR FUN
The Sisters

...⇥

Title: **Smartan Sculpture**
Medium: **Poly**
Credits and Rationale:
**These are the products for the
3rd Anniversary of Smartan.**

⋮

Title: **Adidas ad 01 - 03**
Medium: **Graphic**
Credits and Rationale:
**Smartan is the representative
of Hong Kong's Adidas' perfor-
mance line.**

MY
PERFECT
PERFORMANCE

adidas present

a reni wong's film

coming march 2008

Title: **Bounce fun, bounce hard,
bounce smart**
Medium: **Comics**
Credits and Rationale:
**Smartan is the representative
of Taiwan's Adidas' Bounce line
for magazine ads.**

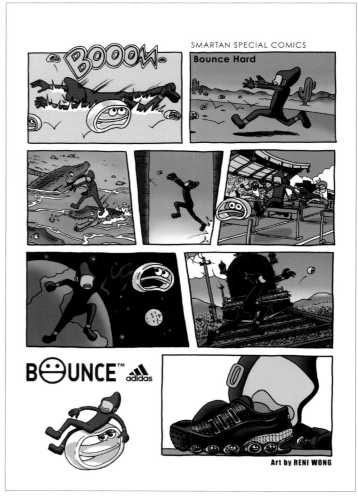

Title: **SStee**
Medium: **T-shirt**
Credits and Rationale:
Smartan Skull limited edition
T-shirts for Smartan Exhibition.

Title: **Cat Pack**
Medium: **Vinyl toy**
Credits and Rationale:
Each of these robot cats has different personalities, a bit weird and unconventional, but they have one mission in common, and that is to fight against evil and to achieve world peace. Catpack comes in a limited edition of four different characters. There are different parts of the body that you can interchange with Catpack.

Title: **Twelve (the Chinese zodiac)**
Medium: **Vinyl Toy**
Credits and Rationale:

A series of 12 oval-shaped characters based on the Chinese zodiac. Reni has given each of these creatures their own unique and wacky personality and created a comic book on the story of how the 12-year cycle of animals came about. There are also two special characters – the Cat and the Jade Emperor.

Cat

Tiger

Rabbit

Mouse

Rooster

Ox

Jade Emperor

Pig

Dog

Dragon

Goat

Monkey

Snake

Horse

THIAGO MANO

Can you please briefly tell us when and how you started "crossover" design? Also how "cross over" design impacted your design style and beliefs at work?

Since I first went to university in 2002, I haven't just been participating in one project. I have many projects and most of them I do in parallel to my work in the agency. I'm always searching for something to do, from illustrations in PixelArt (I love to make pixel to pixel illustrations, even though it may seem crazy!) to projects that were thought up when I was a student and now are more mature and real.

What is your view of the current trend of "crossover" design? For example, will the emergence of "crossover" design make the current separation of work boundaries fuzzy? Why? Will "crossover" affect the professionalism of design work?

I've always worked as a freelancer, doing my artwork and my projects in parallel to my job in the agency. Indeed I believe that my projects improve with the experiences I have with the other projects. I am lucky to work in an agency that also allows me to do personal projects. These are two jobs which are always influencing one another, without preventing the development of both. This way I can do everything at once.

What is your work plan in the future?

I'm not sure what I will do, for example, for the next 5 years. I know it will be related to design. I have projects in progress that I want to bring to maturity, others on paper that I want to materialize.

Name: Thiago Mano
Country: Brazil
Email: thiagomano@gmail.com
Website: www.thiagomano.com
www.flickr.com/thiagomano

Bio:
I am a Portuguese-Brazilian 25 year-old graphic designer. I also illustrate during my down time. I live in Rio de Janeiro, after spending part of my childhood and youth in Portugal. Currently, I work in a communication and events agency as part of its creative team. I have a parallel project – site/ blog about design, called De2ign e-magazine - with my wife and graphic designer, Barbara Formagio.

...›
Title: **PixelArt Leblon Beach**
Medium: **Illustration Design**
Dimension: **200 × 250 mm**
Credits and Rationale:
Illustration in PixelArt

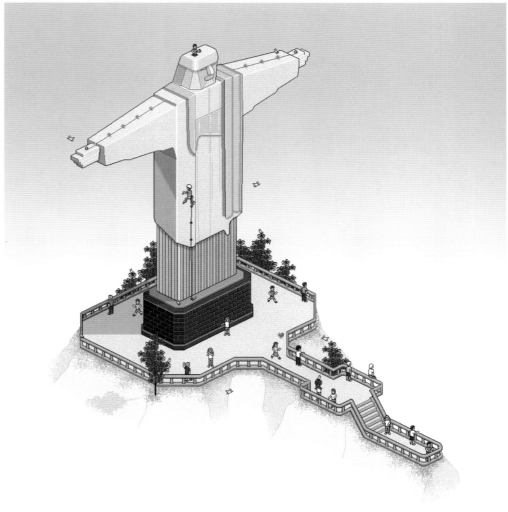

Title: **PixelArt Design Studio**
Medium: **Illustration Design**
Dimension: **420 × 250 mm**
Credits and Rationale:
Illustration in PixelArt.

Title: **PixelArt Design Studio**
Medium: **Illustration Design**
Dimension: **420 × 250 mm**
Creditsand Rationale:
Illustration in PixelArt.

Title: **PixelArt Sunday in the Park**
Medium: **Illustration Design**
Dimension: **420 × 250 mm**
Credits and Rationale:
Illustration in PixelArt.

Title: **PixelArt Corcovado**
Medium: **Illustration Design**
Dimension: **517 × 570 mm**
Credits and Rationale:
Illustration in PixelArt.

...▶
Title: **Vegla Master**
Medium: **Graphic Design**
Dimension: **420 × 250 mm**
Credits and Rationale:
**Create a visual identity of
this Portuguese construction
company with projects in Brazil
and Angola.**

⋮

Title: **Vegla Master**
Medium: **Graphic Design**
Dimension: **276 × 207 mm**
Credits and Rationale:
**Stationery set : envelope,
letterhead, and business card.**

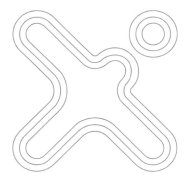

Title: **Xavana Indutra**
Medium: **Fashion Design /
Graphic Design**
Dimension: **420 × 250 mm**
Credits and Rationale:
**Idealization, conceptualization
and creation of the Brazilian
T-shirt collection.**

Title: **Xavana Indutra -
xavanaindutra03.jpg**
Medium: **Fashion Design /
Graphic Design**
Dimension: **276 × 207 mm**
Credits and Rationale:
**Catalog, release invitation card,
and institutional gifts.**

Title: **Xavana Indutra**
Medium: **Fashion Design /
Graphic Design**
Dimension: **420 × 250 mm**
Credits and Rationale:
Brand's construction.

Title: **Xavana Indutra**
Medium: **Fashion Design /
Graphic Design**
Dimension: **276 × 207 mm**
Credits and Rationale:
T-shirts collection release.

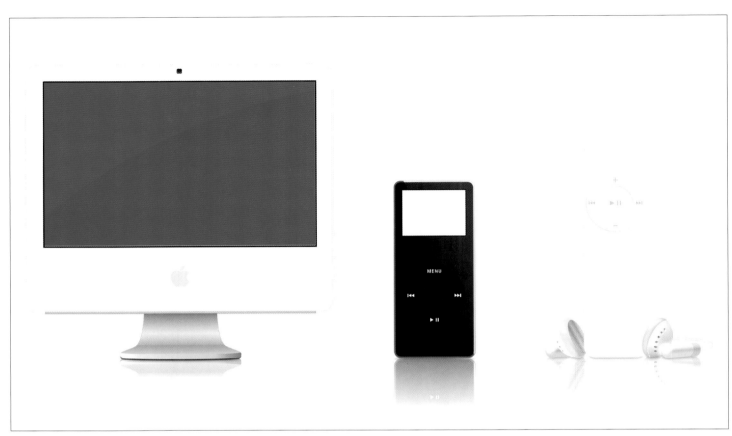

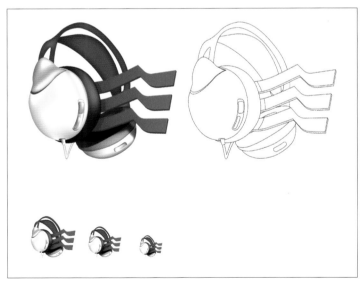

Title: **Apple Products & TIM Music Store**
Medium: **Illustration Design**
Dimension: **420 × 250 mm , 297 × 235 mm**
Credits and Rationale:
Vector illustration of Apple products and icon for TIM Music Store, a company's service in Brazil.

‹⋯

Title: **De2ign eMagazine**
Medium: **Graphic Design**
Dimension: **276 × 207 mm**
Credits and Rationale:
**Brazilian Site/Blog about design,
illustration, photography and
fashion.**

⋮

Title : **Belmont**
Technique : **Design graphique**

...▸

Title: **Lounge of TIM Festival 2008**
Medium: **Interior Design**
Dimension: **276 × 207 mm**
Credits and Rationale:
**Lounge of TIM Festival 2008.
Created and produced by
Conception agency.**

⋮

Title: **Lounge of TIM Festival 2008**
Medium: **Interior Design**
Credits and Rationale:
**Alternating lighting with the
Festival's colours representing
the fire and water elements.
Created and produced by
Conception agency.**

← ···
Title: **Lounge of TIM Festival 2008**
Medium: **Interior Design**
Dimension: **276 × 207 mm**
Credits and Rationale:
Lounge of TIM Festival 2008. Created and produced by Conception agency.

↖ ···
Title: **Lounge of TIM Festival 2008**
Medium: **Interior Design**
Dimension: **276 × 207 mm**
Credits and Rationale:
Lounge of TIM Festival 2008. Created and produced by Conception agency.

↑
Title: **Lounge of TIM Festival 2008**
Medium: **Interior Design**
Dimension: **276 × 207 mm**
Credits and Rationale:
Touch screen projections presenting the previous Festival editions. Created and produced by Conception agency.

← ···
Title: **MasterBag**
Medium: **Graphic Design**
Dimension: **266 × 300 mm**
Credits and Rationale:
Each line has a single tag colour, creating a second identity for each one.

WILLIANS FERNANDES

Can you please briefly tell us when and how you started "crossover" design? Also how "crossover" design impacted your design style and beliefs at work?

COD has been such an inspiration for me and it is giving me the opportunity to show my work abroad. I live in Sao Paulo, Brazil and even though it is a highly urbanized city it is also influenced by graffiti and the underground culture. Being a part of the COD is a very exciting experience and it will be a milestone in my career and personal life. The need to change things runs through the veins of every revolutionary mind. Congratulations and thank you all.

What is your view of the current trend of "crossover" design? For example, will the emergence of "crossover" design make the current separation of work boundaries fuzzy? Why? Will "crossover" affect the professionalism of design work?

I believe COD is doing a very important job of showcasing work and tendencies that are not in the mainstream. Things are always changing and evolving and here we see some people taking the creative mind and vision to the next level. Boldness goes a long way.

What is your work plan in the future?

What do I know about the future at the age of 24? We have very little control over our lives and what lies ahead at that point, but I believe that growing up and getting stronger as a person will reflect and evolve my work as well.

Name: Willians Fernandes
Company: Willportifolio
Country: Brazil
Email: contato@willportifolio.com.br
Web: www.willportifolio.com.br

Bio:
Willians Fernandes, Aka Will, Brazilian designer, illustrator and animator, lives in Sao Paulo, Brazil. Born in 1984 in Sao Paulo, I started my career with 16 years work at a marketing agency that gave me the chance to start my design career, until then I never worked as a creative and I had poor design sense. Before that, I started with publicity agencies and today I work at a marketing agency and also with freelance projects in my free time. In 2008 I was invited to participate with some magazines and book from France, Dubai, Uruguay, and England. I met so many people and artists and to them I dedicate this work.

···▸
Title: **Profession Design**
Medium: **Graphic Design**
Dimension: **420 × 250 mm**
Credits and Rationale:
Work developed for the book Graphic Volcano 2009. This work is very important to me. It expressed the very condition that I was in at the time of creation. Shows the work of a professional and the joy of finalizing a great job.

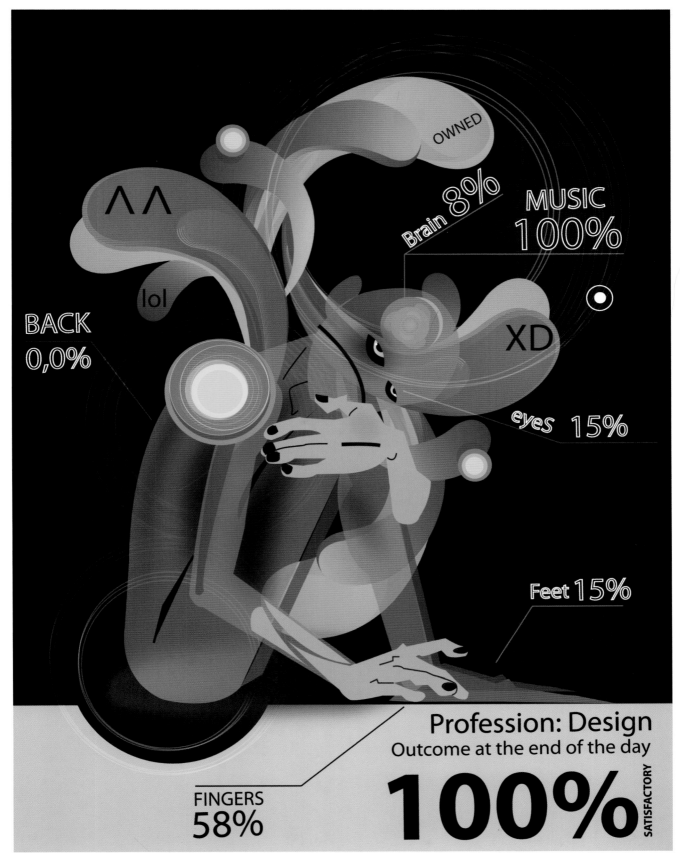

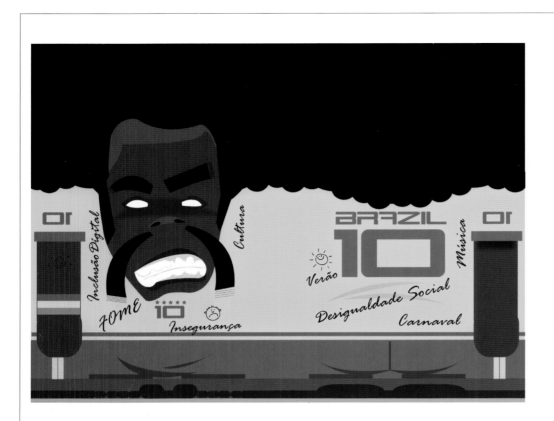

Title: **Brazil**
Medium: **Product Design**
Credits and Rationale:
Work produced for study, the idea was to have a place to put the control of my IMAC.

Title: **Metropole**
Medium: **Graphic Design**
Credits and Rationale:
This work was created to show the new trends of summer 2009 in Brazil.

Title: **Egg Amazing**
Medium: **Graphic Design**
Credits and Rationale:
**This work was created to show
which of the most foreign born
may be the best superheroes.**

Title: **Sk8 T-shirt**
Medium: **Product Design**
Credits and Rationale:
This work was created for a custom T-shirt store. Is art more dedicated to young people. Vibrant colors for the summer of 2008.

...›

Title: **Monster Life**
Medium: **Product Design**
Credits and Rationale:
This work was developed for a skate company. The idea was to represent a young man's shop.

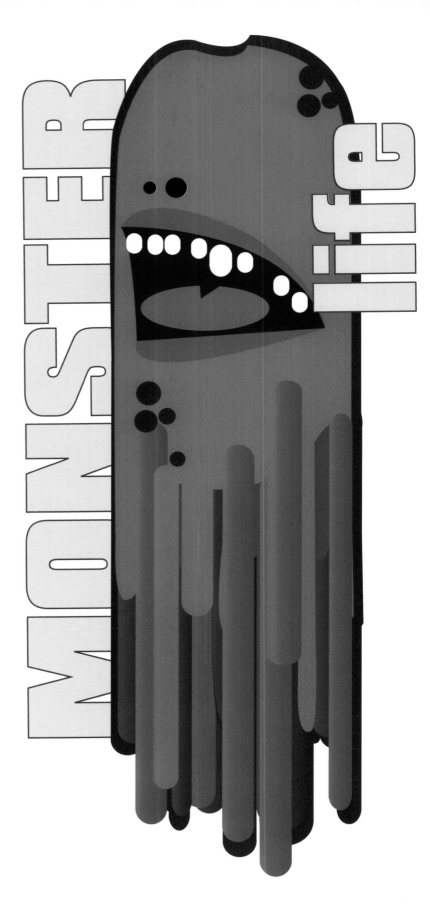

◄┄┄

Title: **Happy Box**
Medium: **Product Design**
Credits and Rationale:
This work was developed for a promotional marketing agency. It was distributed as a gift at year-end for all clients of the company.

⋮

Title: **Freeze Monster Squiizy**
Medium: **Product Design**
Credits and Rationale:
This is a paper toy developed to serve as a promotional year-end gift. It can also serve as a decoration or a simple toy for children or adults.

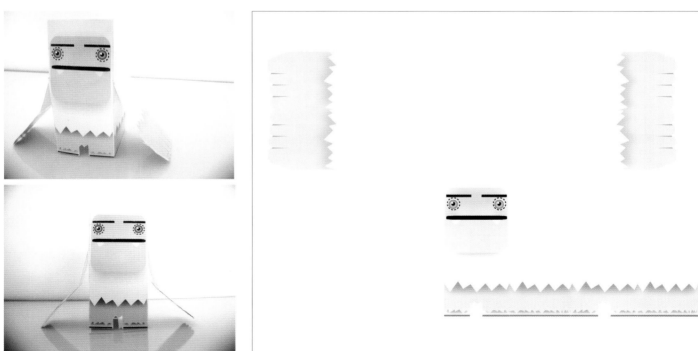

Title: **Surf Championship**
Medium: **Graphic Design**
Credits and Rationale:
**This work was created according
to the concept of a surf shop.
The idea was to change the
entire look of the company.**

Title: **Peace & Love**
Medium: **Graphic Design**
Credits and Rationale:
This study was designed to convey a message of peace to all people. We can believe in peace and learn to respect each citizen. The world needs peace and I wish it for all.

Title: **Sk8board Art**
Medium: **Product Design**
Credits and Rationale:
This work was developed for a skateboard shop in Brazil. The idea was to create a new visual concept for the company's skates.

Title: **Brazilian Art**
Medium: **Graphic Design**
Credits and Rationale:
**This work was inspired by the
Brazilian underground world.
The idea was to show a little
part of urban art of Brazilian
graffiti.**

Title: **Kiss of Hades**
Medium: **Graphic Design**
Credits and Rationale:
This work was created to show time is important in the life of a god, the kiss of death. The time that a name will be chosen and the same will be taken from this world.

Title: **Think About Your Life**
Medium: **Graphic Design**
Credits and Rationale:
The idea of this work and show is that we all need a time to think about our lives and our futures. That it does not always work thoroughly is good for the mind and therefore the idea of this show is that we always need a time to think.

Think about your LIFE every day

NEWWEBPICK.COM
SUPER PICK OF THE WORLD

About NewWebPick.com

NWP (newwebpick.com), founded in 2001, has become one of the most reputable global community platforms for the creative industry. It is difficult today to seek out creative and innovative designs, for there are simply too many designers and portfolios out there in the world. With the internet, it has become easier than ever to showcase one's work and to proclaim oneself as a designer.

As one of the most professional communities in the creative industry, it is our mission to seek, to show, and to recommend all of the most excellent global creative designers. In addition, we also provide a platform for creative professionals, who are willing to show their creative works, to share their inspiration and originality, and welcome any constructive comments from other professionals from all over the world.

About NewWebPick E-magazine

NewWebPick e-magazine, since our first issue came out in 2004, generated 1.8 million readers downloads within a month. Today, our e-magazine has become the world's most distributed e-magazine for the creative industry. Every single edition has attracted more than 4 million readers (independent IP) downloaded from 159 countries, mainly in North America, Europe, South America, China, Southeast Asia, Japan, Korea, the Middle East, and Africa. The readers are mostly highly-qualified professionals between the ages of 22-45, involved or obsessed with new creative-related artwork and lifestyle. 95% of our readers are urban dwellers, from NYC, London, Madrid, Milan, Paris, Tokyo, Seoul, Beijing, Shanghai, Hong Kong, Bangkok, Singapore and other urban centers.

To date, we have published three magazines:

The original magazine, NewWebPick, in each issue has introduced more than 30 designers from all over the world in all kinds of creative art types, such as digital publishing, advertising, product design, industrial design, interior design, photography, Computer Graphic design and animation, illustration, and others.

CONNECTION--we believe there are so many creative talents from every country, and we believe many professionals want to understand difference creative works from difference countries. CONNECTION is a country-specific magazine, and each issue will introduce talents from specific countries to show and demonstrate their creative works more in detail to the rest of the world.

UNIVERSITY DESIGNS (UD) This is a unique platform is offered to art schools, to collaborate their students' great works, showing and telling to the world that "we got talent."

Republic of Designers 52 plus (ReD52+)

ReD52+ is a project conceived by NewWebPick. With a growing community of over 4 million elite designers as NewWebPick readers and contributors, ReD52+ is dedicated to create partnerships with retailers to bridge the gap between designers who deserve notice, and retailers who want exceptional designs.